# Analytic Engagements with Adolescents

In *Analytic Engagements with Adolescents*, Mary T. Brady takes on the intensity and 'heat' of adolescent psychoanalytic treatment. She is a guide in the distinctive challenges of work with adolescents. The intensity of this work manifests in various ways; the heightened importance of body issues and related transference and countertransference, the subversiveness of risk-taking behavior and the rejection and rebellion against authority, and the effects of parental response and family dynamics.

Adolescence is a period when 'things happen': first wet dreams, first menstruation, first romance. Nascent sexuality comes directly into the field as the adolescent is confronted with new bodily experiences. Subversiveness is integral to the adolescent's development; parents (and analysts) are overthrown as the adolescent questions the status quo and experiments with new capacities and desires. Drawn into the adolescent's turbulence, Bion's concept of 'thinking under fire' is shown to be vital to the analyst's engagement. Bion's group theory here informs Brady's immediate experience of the interaction of individual and family dynamics.

The voices of Brady's adolescent patients and her dynamic involvement with them will help the clinician to be open to the 'hot' moments of their analytic work. Drawing on Bion's thinking and her own extensive experience with adolescents, Brady offers an essential guide to the difficulties and challenges encountered when working with this patient group. She provides practical suggestions for psychoanalysts and psychoanalytic psychotherapists working in this area.

**Mary T. Brady** is a psychoanalyst in private practice in San Francisco. She is on the Faculty of the San Francisco Center for Psychoanalysis and author of *The Body in Adolescence: Psychic Isolation and Physical Symptoms* (Routledge: 2016).

'Mary Brady knows very well adolescents and the intensity of the conflicts they face; she captures the essence of the complex and stimulating work of containment and psychoanalytic technique with adolescents. She restores the body issues to a central position and offers rich and radical reflections on working with parents and family dynamics. The complexity of transference and countertransference when working with impulsivity and intensity is explored here and gives rise to fascinating elaborations on psychoanalysis with adolescence. This is a brilliant book, exciting and very accessible: a good combination of education, emotional support, and psychoanalytic thinking.'

– **Christine Anzieu-Premmereur, MD, PhD**, Assistant Clinical Professor in Psychiatry at Columbia University; Director of the Columbia University Psychoanalytic Center's Parent-Infant Program; member of the New York Psychoanalytic Institute

'Mary Brady has done it again. This is a remarkable book about adolescents and Brady's own deep engagements with them and their turbulent or sleepy states. She writes profoundly about the erotic field which emerges and the challenge for psychoanalysts to talk about feelings the adolescent may barely have begun to name. She stresses the importance of monitoring when what she calls "erotic sufficiency" in the analysis can be overstimulating – but she is equally strong on the dangers of erotic insufficiency in the relationship. We all have much to learn from her about how to help patients achieve both intimacy and aliveness.'

– **Anne Alvarez, PhD, MACP**, Consultant Child and Adolescent Psychotherapist

'We should celebrate the publication of this new book by Mary Brady, which takes us directly to the core of psychoanalytic work with adolescents. She invites us into her consulting room, where we witness her meeting with young patients to engage in a work that is hard but immensely gratifying. This is an indispensable book because of its clinical honesty. Dr. Brady has found a way of getting close to her patients without intruding, of containing the anxiety generated in the analytic interaction, of interpreting in a way that is both straightforward and subtle, and, above all, of observing and listening. She does not fail to ponder the current conditions of the context in which adolescents live, a world full of danger and violence where social institutions cannot effectively support the process that teenagers must necessarily undergo.'

– **Virginia Ungar, MD**, IPA President

# Analytic Engagements with Adolescents

Sex, Gender, and Subversion

Mary T. Brady

Routledge
Taylor & Francis Group

LONDON AND NEW YORK

First published 2018
by Routledge
2 Park Square, Milton Park, Abingdon, Oxon OX14 4RN

and by Routledge
711 Third Avenue, New York, NY 10017

*Routledge is an imprint of the Taylor & Francis Group, an informa business*

*British Library Cataloguing in Publication Data*
A catalogue record for this book is available from the British Library

*Library of Congress Cataloging in Publication Data*
A catalog record for this book has been requested

ISBN: 978-0-8153-8322-2 (hbk)
ISBN: 978-0-8153-8323-9 (pbk)
ISBN: 978-1-351-20631-0 (ebk)

Typeset in Times New Roman
by Swales & Willis Ltd, Exeter, Devon, UK

For Danny

# Contents

# Foreword

Not everyone loves working with adolescents. Some of them defy, provoke and taunt us. Some merely worry us from time to time, while others leave us fearing for their lives. They put us on the spot, get under our skin. They summon ghosts from our own years as teens, stirring memories and feelings that may unsettle and freshly confound us. Not everyone welcomes the challenges of analytic work with adolescents, with its unique intensity and intimacy, but Mary Brady clearly does. Her love for the work is evident on every page of this book.

As you'll see, she has a talent for making complex theoretical concepts accessible in everyday language without resorting to convoluted academic jargon or clichés. Reading her, you hear her voice – a very natural, direct voice – as if she's sharing what she's learned with a trusted friend. What comes through is what's essential, a breath of fresh air.

There's plenty of heat in the book, too – associated first with what Brady refers to as "the developing adolescent erotic body and mind," and manifest clinically in erotic transference and countertransference. She explores this terrain with keen attention to the body and to the adolescent's nascent kindling of love and desire. With 'Frank,' a 12-year-old boy who might have been frightened by too-intense scrutiny of his feelings for her, Brady's comments are a model of delicacy and tact. She acknowledges what she perceives him to feel, while making it clear that it's safe to talk about such feelings because they won't be acted upon. When she adds, "I wouldn't want you to think such feelings are weird," it's more than a fleeting reassurance. Subtly, she's referencing a developmental context in which his feelings are natural and not to be feared, thereby inviting him to explore his inner life more freely. In this and many other clinical vignettes, we see her gift for addressing profound and sometimes urgent matters with a light and graceful touch.

You won't find a trace of orthodoxy here. No guidelines, no truisms, no oversimplifications. Intellectually, Brady is an explorer: curious, questioning, intrigued by the unusual and the unknown. It's no surprise that she appreciates adolescent experimentation with respect to identity in its full complexity, or that she celebrates the flowering of creativity rooted in adolescent subversiveness; hers is a kindred spirit.

At the Wright Institute, where we met as students more than 30 years ago, many of our faculty were inspired by Critical Theory and its emphasis on dialectical inquiry. For instance, our fairly traditional Psychopathology course was followed immediately by Social Psychopathology, its full-semester critique. Brady credits this atmosphere of in-depth scholarship and lively, provocative debate as a lasting influence.

In this collection you'll also see her affinities with Winnicott and Bion, whose thinking she blends artfully with her own. You'll encounter her unique versions of *gremlins* and *sleeping beauties* – the former referring to unexpected and disconcerting "'mechanical failures' of erections, sleep or speech" that she associates with a stultifying ideal of masculinity; the latter, to seemingly placid adolescents who appear to be "sleeping through or forestalling the separation process" essential to their individuation.

To me, perhaps the finest jewel in this collection is her paper "'Sometimes we are prejudiced against ourselves": internalized and external homophobia in the treatment of an adolescent boy.' I'm moved by the beauty of the clinical work and I admire the candor and sensitivity with which she explores a developmental domain too long neglected in our literature. *Analytic Engagements with Adolescents: Sex, Gender, and Subversion* contains much to inspire us and to stimulate fresh thought. It's the work of a consummate clinician sharing the fruits of a creative mind and a wise and generous heart.

Christina Halsey
Oakland, California

# Acknowledgments

A second book, like a second baby, is easier. The mysteries of book publishing have receded and the fear of having nothing to say is easier to beat back. In fact, I continue to feel that there is much to say about adolescents, who can be riveting, evocative and touching.

Chief amongst colleagues to thank are Ray Poggi and Robert Tyminski. Ray has been my most important mentor for many years. Such a relationship is one of the great good fortunes of life. For a decade now, Robert and I have taught a weekly consultation group on the treatment of adolescents and young adults. This group has been a central part of my on-going clinical, intellectual and emotional life. I have been grateful for the wisdom, insight and humour Robert brings to co-leading the group. I have also been grateful to the group members who have long nourished my thinking: Jacquie Ward, Dawn Smith, Kristen Carey, Michael Loeffler, Jeremy Marshman, Danni Biondini and Michael Wachter are the current members. Robert and my pleasure with this first group led to a new consultation group this year. It has been a pleasure to deepen relationships with members of this group and hear from new and talented voices: Karen Dozer, Kevin Hibbit, Kelsey Parker, Mara Dubey, Charles Fritz and Zoe Strauss.

I am also grateful to Diane Borden – film scholar and friend. She and I launched the Adolescents on Film group in 2016. The wonderful films and the colleagues who people the group are sources of growth and stimulation. Those colleagues are Carol Cunningham, Eric Essman, Lauren Ores Phillips, Sandra Salatich, Meryl Botkin, Candis Cousins, Elissa Meryl, Dorian Newton and Michael Wachter.

Two valued senior colleagues, Virginia Ungar and Donald Moss, have contributed to this book by their thinking and their generosity. My friends Christina Halsey, Cathy Witzling, Sharon Tyson, Jacquie Ward,

Dawn Smith, Catherine Mallouh, Cheryl Goodrich, Margo Chapin, Til Stewart and Holly Gordon enliven and enrich my life, my clinical thinking and my writing. Patricia Marra, friend and colleague, made a particular contribution in editing some of the chapters.

Finally, I am grateful to my son Danny for his belief in me, for the fine young man he has become and for how much his father's vitality shines through in him.

# Introduction

## Hot topics: analytic engagements with adolescents

I have often wondered about my enduring interest in analytic work with adolescents, and have even questioned if it is masochistic, since at times they can be so peculiarly difficult (e.g., patients who won't speak to you, patients who mock you, patients who disregard analytic rules and so-called decorum, patients who are frequently on the verge of needing more help than our relationship can offer). I have thought about what I am reworking from my own adolescence – suffice it to say that I feel a certain protectiveness of the adolescent process. However, I believe there are intrinsic elements that make the treatment of adolescents such a distinct experience.

First, the body of the adolescent and the body of the analyst are the subjects of analysis in a more urgent way than is the case in treating younger children or adults. I could imagine a reader thinking, is that really so? What about the young child's body? I picture a seven-year-old who had a near-death experience when he was three. During sessions he fell on the floor, feigning death. In play we explored "Am I dead or not?" Surely, his bodily experience was an important aspect of his treatment. Or what about adult patients who massively somatize? One of my patients gained 100 lbs. after I was out for two weeks for a medical procedure (successfully treated with no sequelae). Her bodily communication was certainly in the room in a powerful way (she unconsciously feared that she had caused my medical problem by her voracious need of me). Bodily experience is important at any age, but I will argue that the body of the adolescent patient and the body of analyst are particularly urgent subjects of analysis.

Lombardi (2017: 112) suggests: "[T]he adolescent's mind does not know the body in which it lives, but must discover it." This discovery occurs in many ways, including within the relationship with the analyst.[1] The experiences of puberty and the nascence of sexuality can lead to especially charged erotic transferences and countertransferences. Many years ago, a colleague and I started a consultation group on the treatment of adolescents because of the particular intensities of this work and the resultant need for a thinking group. Erotic longings or suicidal tendencies (for example) are a strain for any analyst to bear. This is intensified in the treatment of adolescents. The analyst of an adolescent bears great responsibility because the patient is not a full adult, yet has many adult choices.

A lesser, but still significant reason that the patient's body and the analyst's body are more central in the treatment of adolescents is that children and adolescents' physical use of the room allows for a different intimacy. Most adult patients lie on our couches and sit in our chairs and talk to us. Some adolescents also do this. Adolescents who have already been in treatment at the end of latency use the office and me in a different manner. A traditional Freudian supervisor told me years ago that she sat at the play table with children and always remained in that seat, making it easier to interpret a child's comings and goings in relation to her. Although I see the point of this, I find it too constraining. A teen might be stretched out on the floor and I might be sitting on the floor nearby. Balls are thrown for me to catch (literally and figuratively). Even sitting together and drawing at the table is closer and more interactive than is the case with adults. A teen might also show me her new hip-hop moves or another teen might bring his skateboard for me to admire. Alvarez (2012) describes an 11-year-old girl showing her a dance the older girls at school were doing:

> Her dancing gave me a new pleasure – she seemed much softer, more shy and less defended than usual. The dancing was modest, but the lightness, grace and yet sexiness were very attractive, and I'm sure my eyes and face – and my words revealed my pleasure and appreciation of this new Nicola. (I said something like "What a lovely dance!")
>
> (128–129)

When children and adolescents are deeply involved in treatment, they feel like they own the room and the analyst's body. (One early teen suggested I get a tropical fish tank for the office.) Of course, there are limits to this. But while generally one goes through a whole analysis with an adult without ever touching her, the use of the space and the physical contact, albeit limited, with an adolescent can create a palpable intimacy. There may be a tousled head leaning over to draw near me that I'd feel like patting. Such tender feelings are certainly part of the analyses of adults, but the physical proximity with children and adolescents intensifies these feelings.

Adolescence takes place in *real time*, and it is a phase when *things happen* – the first wet dream, the beginning of menstruation, the first boyfriend, the first job, getting drunk or high for the first time, etc. The events of adolescence may be remembered or evoked in the treatment of adults,[2] but rarely with the same immediacy.

Another 'hot' aspect of working with teens is that subversion is more central and necessary for adolescents than is the case with younger children and adults. The family is subverted, the analyst is subverted, as the adolescent finds her own sexuality and her own ideas. This fact leads to particular rejections as the roles we have had with adolescents are shifted or toppled. Adolescent risk-taking behavior (which can be a part of the provocation of parental figures) raises unique transference-countertransference interactions and challenges. The adolescent can and should expect a requisite protectiveness from adults, yet the adolescent can throw her lack of concern for her own safety in the analyst or parent's face. Identity is experimented with and renegotiated as this happens.

Challenging transference/countertransference scenarios ensue when parents (intentionally or unintentionally) vacate aspects of parental functioning with adolescents. While we may feel deeply for an adult patient who has been neglected, working with an adolescent left far too much to themselves by parents is highly demanding of analysts both practically and emotionally. It is, of course, extremely painful to treat a young child who is neglected, abused or pathologically projected into. However, there are issues particular to adolescence – such as the adolescent's need to reject or provoke the parent(s),[3] that parents (who previously were reasonably available) can respond to with exhaustion and withdrawal.

Another 'hot' aspect of adolescent treatment is the fact that the adolescent is directly involved with her parents in a day-to-day way, and the analyst is let in on the private life of the family. This leads to particular countertransference experiences of intimacy and voyeurism. For instance, an adolescent boy told me recently of three different incidences in which he had walked in on or overheard his parents having sex. The scene depicted was of parents passionately in love with each other, which this boy found overwhelming. The same memories could have been replayed in the treatment of an adult. However, in some sense I, too, have now walked in on the parents – it is a very hot contact, when I hear such a story and then shortly afterwards meet with these parents (with my own reactions to their passion).

## Comments on the organization of this book

I intend here a series of largely clinical essays to convey distinctive aspects of analytic work with adolescents. In order to preserve the confidentiality of patients, I have changed biographical information and other details throughout this book.

The first three chapters convey the special intensities of treatment involving the adolescent's developing erotic body and mind.

Chapter 1 describes the heightened importance of the body of the adolescent and the body of the analyst and the heat of the erotic transference and countertransference in work with some adolescents. I will convey a period of erotic transference-countertransference in the analysis of an early adolescent boy. Atkinson and Gabbard point out how "sparse" the psychoanalytic literature is "with regard to erotic transference of male adolescent patients to their female analysts" (1995: 173). Needless to say, the discussion of erotic countertransference in this dyad is even sparser.

I then turn in Chapter 2 to the painful experiences of a gay adolescent boy in analytically-oriented psychotherapy. I employ this boy's experience to consider the effects of homophobia, their internalization and their entanglement with intra-psychic processes in adolescence. We all swim in the waters of culture, including our shared theoretical cultures. How can we be sensitive to an adolescent's emerging sexual identity while keeping an eye to prejudice in the culture, in theory and as internalized by patient and analyst?

Chapter 3 explores the avoidance of adolescent turbulence or 'heat' as a not-unusual defensive reaction to the phase. This avoidance can, though, become entrenched and restrict emotional growth. I use the Brothers Grimm's *Sleeping Beauty* to examine the meanings underlying a 'somnolent' picture in adolescence. I consider an absence of passion, including in the analytic process, to be characteristic of the avoidance of developmental turbulence. The analyst may need to allow such an adolescent to be 'somnolent' for some time, but may eventually want to wake him or her (metaphorically) or even pierce the somnolent, avoidant state.

I use clinical vignettes of late adolescents to demonstrate such transitions. This chapter conveys adolescent turbulence in inverse – too hot to handle and thus slept through.

In Chapter 4, I consider 'ideals' of masculinity for boys and men and the potential for these ideals (in their extremity) to contribute to rigid psychic states and splitting. Split-off parts can return through 'gremlin-like' symptoms. These symptoms are subjectively experienced as trouble-making, particularly in relation to being 'big' or 'macho' physically or intellectually. Women or girls who identify with such ideals are also vulnerable to these gremlin-like symptoms. A literary example of an adolescent in David Mitchell's semi-autobiographical novel *Black Swan Green* is offered as well as personal reflections of two analysts, Donald Moss and myself. Negotiation of masculinity can be particularly fraught in adolescence as variations from accepted norms can be severely punished by the group.

Chapter 5 explores the refreshingly radical aspect of adolescent subversiveness. I first contrast subversiveness with rebelliousness in its more satiric and questioning quality. I suggest that adolescent subversiveness is related to the gradual development towards an adult capacity for independence of mind.

I then turn to Bionian approaches to the treatment of adolescents and for work with parents of adolescents in Chapters 6 and 7. Although Bion did not himself treat adolescents, I consider his ideas to be particularly useful in the treatment of adolescents. Bion's suggestion that the analyst needs to be able to interpret 'under fire' is particularly apt in the treatment of adolescents.

Chapter 6 examines Bion's interrelated concepts such as K and -K, container/contained, maternal reverie and the development of thinking through alpha function in relation to adolescent treatment. I discuss Bion's conceptualization of thinking and non-thinking states (K and -K links) through the treatment of a 16-year-old-girl as well as through the treatment of a younger child. I consider how parents sometimes wish to shield their children from important truths. The fear that emotional knowledge will be too painful to bear can interfere with 'learning from experience.'

In the final chapter, I discuss hot issues and challenges in working with parents of adolescents in treatment. Bion's theories regarding unconscious functioning within groups are particularly useful for understanding progressive and regressive shifts within families. The concepts of *work group* and *basic assumption* modes in family groups are examined, as are *group mentality* and *group culture*. I provide clinical examples of work with parents of adolescents (and some younger children).

## Acknowledgment

The Introduction is partly based on: Brady, M.T. (2009). Hot topics: Analytic engagements with adolescents, *fort da, 15*: 57–71. Reprinted by kind permission of the journal.

## Notes

1 Lombardi and I agree about the centrality of the body in adolescence, but differ in certain aspects of technique. Lombardi emphasizes focusing interventions on the patient's relationship with his body and avoiding interpretations within the transference, which he believes adolescents find intrusive. My view is that comments about the adolescent's bodily experience or about the relationship with the analyst can be intrusive or sensitively gauged. The analyst's effort is to foster an open-ended, unsaturated quality of interaction with the adolescent, whether addressing the adolescent's immediate experience of her body or how the experience of the body resides within the relationship with the analyst and others, as well as related aspects of fantasy. The analyst must attend to whether comments about the adolescent's body or transference comments are experienced as intrusive, over-stimulating, avoidant, etc.

2 Blos, Jr. (1990) contends that the events of adolescence are often minimized in adult analyses because of their disturbing affective components. For instance, a pubertal girl conveyed to me how bizarre she felt when she began to get hair under one arm but not yet the other.

3 Traditional developmental theory posits the need for "object removal" (Katan, 1951) in adolescence, particularly of incestuous strivings reactivated by pubertal changes. This process of psychic removal or mourning allows a second individuation process (Blos, 1967). These psychic recalibrations are accomplished only with much psychic distress for the adolescent and her parents. Adolescents are bearing an onslaught of feelings never before or since experienced with the same intensity (Kulish, 1998) – which requires a great deal of the analyst to attempt to traverse this territory with them.

## References

Alvarez, A. (2012). Types of sexual transference and countertransference in work with children and adolescents. In *The Thinking Heart: Three Levels of Psychoanalytic Therapy with Disturbed Children*. Hove and New York: Routledge, Chapter 9, 116–129.

Atkinson, S., & Gabbard, G. (1995). Erotic transference in the male adolescent–female analyst dyad. *Psychoanalytic Study of the Child, 50*: 171–186.

Blos, Sr., P. (1967). The second individuation process of adolescence. *Psychoanalytic Study of the Child, 22*: 162–186.

Blos, Jr., P. (1990). Adolescent fixation in adult psychopathology. In S. Dowling (Ed.), *Child and adolescent analysis: Its significance for clinical work with adults*. Madison, IN: Indiana University Press, pp. 67–79.

Katan, A. (1951). The role of 'displacement' in agoraphobia. *International Journal of Psychoanalysis, 32*: 42–50.

Kulish, N. (1998). First loves and prime adventures: Adolescent expressions in adult analyses. *Psychoanalytic Quarterly, 67*(4): 539–565.

Lena, F.E. (2017). Working with and 'seeing through': Sexual transference in the psychotherapy of an adolescent boy. *Journal of Child Psychotherapy, 43*(1): 40–54.

Lombardi, R. (2017). Body and mind in adolescence. In *Body–Mind Dissociation in Psychoanalysis: Development After Bion*. Abingdon and New York: Routledge, pp. 110–127.

# Chapter 1

# Braving the erotic field in the treatment of adolescents

I have found my patient's body – and my body – to be more directly the subjects of analysis with adolescents than with adults or with younger children. Erotic transference and countertransference can be particularly fraught because of the intensity of emergent bodily sensations in the adolescent and because of her or his normal developmental immaturity. Adolescents need help to name and integrate their newfound bodily experiences. Their minds need to grow into the bodies they now inhabit. It is a challenge for analysts to talk about feelings the adolescent may have barely begun to name. Indeed, budding sexuality and the memories and feelings it stirs in us of our own sexual beginnings are no small things to metabolize. And yet, with rare exceptions, the area of erotic transference/ countertransference in the treatment of adolescents is largely ignored in analytic writing.[1]

The catastrophic prospect of boundary violations, particularly with minors, can lead to a timid avoidance of the erotic in our work with adolescents, yielding what I term an 'erotic insufficiency.' The analyst can fear exploiting the trust necessary for an adolescent to bring his or her emerging sexuality into analysis in a lively manner. Feelings that arouse the greatest conflict and guilt in the analyst are precisely those that are most vulnerable to our defensive rejection. In order to consider these ideas, I will relate a period in the analysis of a 12-year-old boy when the erotic transference and countertransference were at a height. I will also suggest that the terms *erotic transference* and *erotic counter-transference* do not fully capture the intensely interactional nature of these experiences. I suggest *erotic field* better conveys this fluidity.

Erotic transferences and countertransferences with younger children can seem comparatively comfortable.[2] One eight-year-old boy fantasized that he was a king and I his golden-haired queen, living in a castle together, and that we would never have to part. While the scene I'm describing is only the most conscious aspect of a deeper fantasy, I believe that there are also other reasons why my countertransference response was comparatively easy to bear. I could feel the poignancy of this idyllic picture, and sympathize with my patient's frustrations at the inescapable realities of life, such as how old one is, and how old are one's analyst, mother, father, etc. – and how much these exigencies determine. In this familiar oedipal scene, one cannot have what one wants and yet it is better to have wanted it and even to tolerate knowing that one has wanted it. But it was also my younger patient's age and related physical immaturity that contributed to a less charged erotic transference/countertransference than with adolescent patients.

## Changing bodies, changing minds

The body of the adolescent is changing radically before his or her own eyes, as well as mine. Adolescent boys can shoot up a foot in height over a couple of years. 'Brian,' age 13, encountered me in the hallway before a session and said: "Have you always been that short?" His body was new in many ways, and led to new experiences in relation to himself, me and everyone else. Brian and I experienced together his pubertal development and the meanings it shifted within our relationship.

'Naomi,' a pubertal girl, having had the puberty/sex talk at school that day, came to her session and asked me with utter sincerity: "What's puberty for?" I was struck that though I could answer the question in a limited biological sense, the larger psychological and emotional meanings would take years to comprehend.

'Evelyn,' a 16-year-old in analysis, spoke about being on the verge of having intercourse with her boyfriend. I asked her: "Do you think having sex will change anything inside you or between us?" At first she demurred, but soon said: "Having intercourse will be the end of childhood." Something would definitively change inside her, as well as between us, and between her and her parents. She would cross a line from her child bodily self to an adult bodily self and there would no longer be a substantive divide between her experiences and those of adults in a sexual sense. Experience would be gained, but a precious boundary that allowed some element of childhood to remain (all too scarce for this girl) would be lost.

Around this time Evelyn asked to use the couch. Her 'use' of the couch[3] was different than any I have experienced. She was in constant motion and reminded me of a seal. She would flip from side to side and then flip over on her stomach to look at me. My experience was of not being able to think with all this motion and I wished Evelyn would just lie still. Evelyn was giving me an experience of how much commotion she felt at this phase.

Evelyn asked to use the couch in order to talk about sexuality. My agreement for her to lie down evoked intimate and erotic feelings in her toward me. Soon after starting to use the couch she told me of making out with her boyfriend in his car for the first time. She said: "I found myself tracing your initials in the steam on the window." As we explored this action it seemed that I was both present in Evelyn's erotic feelings *and* that she was summoning me to help her create some 'brakes' to allow thinking space while making out with her boyfriend.

In all of these instances, the teens were experiencing rapid bodily changes that they brought to analysis for consideration. I will turn briefly to erotic transference and countertransference in the psychoanalytic literature on adults in order to create a backdrop from which to consider the far more scant literature on transference/countertransference with adolescent patients.

## Erotic transference and countertransference in the adult literature

Person (1985) defines "erotic transference" as interchangeable with "transference love," meaning "some mixture of tender, erotic, and sexual feelings that a patient experiences in reference to his or her analyst and, as such, forms part of a positive transference" (Person, 1985: 161).[4] She describes the erotic transference as "both goldmine and minefield" (1985: 163). Passionate feelings are likely to be confusing to patient and analyst and thus their consideration can yield great rewards. Simultaneously, intense feelings in the patient or analyst are also prone to either some form of acting out or defensive avoidance.

A patient's erotic feelings toward an analyst can sometimes be intensely driven and even psychotic in the Kleinian sense of losing touch with reality. Blum describes "eroticized transference" as a "particular species of erotic transference, an extreme sector of a spectrum. It is an intense, vivid, irrational, erotic preoccupation with the analyst, characterized by overt, seemingly ego-syntonic demands for love and sexual fulfillment from the analyst" (1973: 63). In my experience there are patients who waver between a *capacity* to allow strong feelings toward their analyst without becoming psychotic but who may lose hold of reality considerations in the throes of intense feelings.

Person points out that (even in the adult literature) erotic transference "has always been tainted by unsavory associations and continues to be thought of as slightly disreputable" (1985: 163) compared with analytic reflection on other forms of transference. In a sense this is strange, as Freud struggled mightily (in introducing his concept of infantile sexuality) to help us see that there are intense and passionate forces in us all from the beginning. And yet, perhaps we have to accept that passionate and deeply rooted forces always create some defensive alarm. How much more so when the patient has not reached adulthood?

In a well-known and groundbreaking paper, Searles (1958) squares off against the orthodox notion, prevalent at the time, that intense emotional reactions on the part of the analyst are pathological:

> [I]n the course of a successful psychoanalysis, the analyst goes through a phase of reacting to, and eventually relinquishing, the patient as being his oedipal love-object; (b) in normal personality development, the parent reciprocates the child's oedipal love with greater intensity than we have recognized heretofore; and (c) in such normal development the passing of the Oedipus Complex is at least as important a phase in ego-development as in superego development.
>
> (180)

Racker (1953) likewise contends that the Oedipus Complex will express itself in every countertransference, while the form, consciousness of it and intensity vary:

> [S]ometimes the analyst loves the patient genitally and desires her genital love towards him; he hates her if she then loves another man, feels rivalry of this man and jealousy and envy (heterosexual and homosexual) of their sexual pleasure. Sometimes he hates her if she hates him, and loves her if she suffers, for in this case he is revenged for the oedipic deceit. He feels satisfaction when the transference is very positive, but also castration anxiety and guilt feelings toward the husband, etc.
>
> (316)

I am using *countertransference* here to denote the analyst's experience of an intensely interactional transference-countertransference dialogue (Greenberg & Mitchell, 1983; Langs, 1981; Little, 1951; Ogden, 1997; Racker, 1957; Searles, 1958; Winnicott, 1949).[5]

## Erotic transference and countertransference, adolescent style

Lena, in a paper discussing the erotic transference of a 16-year-old boy to his female therapist, contends:

> Given the centrality of sexual impulses and fantasies in adolescence, one would think that the erotic transference is a common phenomenon in many therapists with adolescents . . . When discussing this topic with colleagues working with adolescents most psychotherapists could think of cases when powerful sexual feelings coloured the transference relationship. And yet little has been written about the erotic transference in childhood and adolescence, even less about the experience of the therapist.
>
> (2016: 43)

Atkinson and Gabbard likewise comment: "[E]rotic material in an adolescent's transference may create in the analyst a level of concern or even fear of parental retaliation should the parents become aware of the material" (1995: 174). I would add that the fear of the parents' potential response can also be a projection of the analyst's own parental superego, which can lead to repression or avoidance.

Alvarez's (2012) paper 'Types of sexual transference and countertransference in work with children and adolescents' is a rare and substantive contribution to this topic. She distinguishes amongst "perverse," "disordered" and "normal" sexual transferences in children and adolescents. *Perverse* denotes a dangerously addictive sexuality with sadistic and masochistic elements. *Disordered* indicates an addictive but not fully perverse sexuality. And by *normal* Alvarez implies the child or adolescent's desire "to make someone's eyes light up" (2012: 126) and "the need for a responsive interested object capable of being delighted" (2012: 126).

Paton discusses a scenario when an adolescent sexualizes the therapeutic atmosphere to "avoid feelings of unhappiness and vulnerability"

(2017: 28), which would be similar to Blum's description of eroticized transference and could overlap with Alvarez's perverse or disordered sexual transferences.

Jackson (a male analyst) describes an 18-year-old woman's adjustment to the couch:

> For the first few weeks Sarah seemed tense, lying on the couch with her knees up as if she felt like a terrified virgin on her wedding night. This was poignantly represented when she told me how her new travel card gave her freedom to go wherever she wanted but left her worrying about whether she could manage the increased cost. She was able to recognize how the 'cost' in the transference connected in part to the increased access she had to her fantasies about my 'private life' and her hatred of feeling so excluded from it.
>
> (2017: 18)

Jackson (2017) warns that when sexuality emerges within the transference and countertransference with our adolescent patients, "threatening to disrupt our thinking and shatter our psychic equilibrium . . . we should not underestimate our propensity to avoid, negate and defend ourselves against these dynamics, even when we are conscious of them" (2017: 6). He notes that it can be difficult to distinguish between being safe and containing of our adolescent patients' erotic feelings and "something that is rationalized as safe and containing but which is essentially evasive and defensive on the part of the therapist" (2017: 12). Similarly, Atkinson and Gabbard (1995) describe an erotic transference of a male patient with a female therapist and note that the therapist in such a pairing may be tempted to overemphasize maternal feelings.

Just as we may be avoidant of erotic feelings in clinical work with adolescents, we also seem to be avoidant of these feelings in clinical writing. Jackson notes that while the analytic literature on erotic transference and countertransference with adults is thin, "it is especially thin in relation to psychoanalytic work with children and adolescents" (2017: 8).

Adolescent treatment requires a freedom to experience and tolerate intense feelings, while attempting to be neither over-stimulating nor neglectful of sexual feelings. The following vignette is an excellent example of this. Jackson describes Sarah, an 18-year-old who he sometimes feels to be the "apple of my eye" (2017: 18). Sarah tells her analyst she has kissed a close friend of her boyfriend.

> The intensity of the impact this had on me was startling. I experienced it like a personal assault – a body blow, affecting my whole physiology and evoking something not far off a sense of outrage as if she had actually been unfaithful to me.
>
> (2017: 18)

The intensity of Jackson's reaction jarred him and gradually led him to understand that Sarah had experienced their recent agreement for her to use the couch as a sexual enactment. Jackson's subsequent vacation break thus felt like a betrayal to her. As he reflected on his intense reaction mentioned above Jackson became more active in interpreting how his breaks "could feel like a violation of the therapy and the therapeutic relationship" (2017: 18). Sarah then tells him that she had kissed the boy to hurt him more than her boyfriend. Jackson replies:

> I acknowledged the importance of what she was saying about how angry, jealous and cheated on she felt by me over Easter, adding that perhaps now I needed to know what that was like – including what it was like to feel sexually jealous.
>
> (2017: 18)

Jackson keeps a close eye to the effect of his comments on his patient. While always important, this close attunement to how our words are experienced is only more important in this erotic territory – over-stimulating or insufficient?

## Erotic Insufficiency/Erotic Playback

The emerging bodily experiences of the adolescent (first menstruation, first wet dream, first masturbation to orgasm, etc.) are parts of a "virgin territory" (Holtzman & Kulish, 1997; Kulish, 1998). For the analyst, the patient's pubertal development can rouse feelings of venturing into a particularly forbidden, loaded and vulnerable area. This can create hesitancy and inhibition in the analyst, making her less likely to be able to stand for the acceptance and containment of these sensations and emotions.

Samuels (a post-Jungian analyst) suggests that

> the subtle damage and deprivation caused by erotic deficit is far less
> spoken of than what is caused by erotic excess. Physical incest takes
> place at an appallingly high frequency . . . but something equally cen-
> tral and much more benevolent in sexuality is being overlooked.
>
> (2000: 278)

I prefer the term 'erotic insufficiency' as 'deficit' implies a lack of capacity, while therapists' avoidance of the erotic with adolescents is often
caused more by discomfort and anxiety than incapacity.

Samuels describes "erotic playback" (2000: 277) in parenting and in
clinical processes:

> [I]n the family this is the way in which the parent communicates to
> children of both sexes that they are admirable, physically desirable
> and erotically viable creatures. Of course, in a family or in analysis I
> am referring only to incest fantasy and not to the physical enactment
> of such fantasy.
>
> (2000: 277)

Samuels adds that the erotic includes more than sex; it also encompasses
"harmony, relatedness, purpose, significance, and meaning Eros . . . This
means of course, that ambivalence, anxiety, jealousy, rivalry, and a sense
of lack will also be present" (2000: 278). To translate into my Bionian
clinical language – an analyst would need to be emotionally responsive and
containing to the erotic (in a broad sense) and also to the related subtleties
and problems: what's too much? What's too remote or defensive? What is
hard to bear about the erotic? What is enlivening or even transformative?

Samuels' concept of erotic playback is not simplistic. He sees sexual
identity as not "unified, fixed, static, eternal, universal" (2000: 278).
Erotic playback encourages the individual "to think of himself or herself
in a diversified way, to come alive and hold together in the mind all
aspects of the self – body areas, mental areas" (2000: 278). Samuels
acknowledges that erotic playback is vulnerable to mis-attunement as well
as to more egregious failures.

Ogden's work on the "aliveness" of the analytic exchange broadly
approximates what Samuels is describing. Ogden advocates the analyst's

"spontaneity and freedom to respond to the analysand from his own experience in the analytic situation in a way that is not strangulated by stilted caricatures of analytic neutrality" (1995, p. 696). He says:

> I believe that every form of psychopathology represents a specific type of limitation of the individual's capacity to be fully alive as a human being. The goal of analysis from this point of view is larger than that of the resolution of unconscious intrapsychic conflict, the diminution of symptomatology, the enhancement of reflective subjectivity and self-understanding, and the increase of sense of personal agency. Though one's sense of being alive is intimately intertwined with each of the above-mentioned capacities, I believe that the experience of aliveness is a quality that is superordinate to these capacities.
>
> (1995: 696)

More specific to the present discussion, Elise discusses "analytic eroticism": the "aesthetic capacity to keep . . . embodied vitality alive in the analytic relationship" (2017: 34). She compares analytic eroticism to Kristeva's (2014) discussion of maternal eroticism: "[T]he encounter with the mother as erotic being brings into being the child's erotic self, both in the specifically sexual and in the most general sense: vitality in living, a curious and creative engagement with life – Eros" (Elise, 2017: 34). A simple and lovely example comes to mind. Seven-year-old Spencer comes to his session dressed in a collared shirt instead of his usual tee shirts. He tells me that it had been 'picture day' at school and that his mother told him he was wearing his 'handsome' shirt. How beautifully, naturally and subtly she was sowing the seeds of his developing sense as an attractive and desirable boy and future man.

As parents or analysts we do not often consciously set out to provide our children or patients 'erotic playback.' But perhaps we have trouble naming that along with the growth of the mind, we also hope to help free the growth of erotic aliveness in our patients – both sexually and in related forms, such as a passion for ideas, rich sensuality and a broad and complex range of emotional experience and expressiveness.

Timid avoidance of erotic feelings in the consulting room deprives adolescents of sincere adult thinking in relation to allowing and managing sexual feelings. The analyst's capacity to be aware of their erotic feelings but not to act on them comes across in many ways. If the analyst can feel some ease with sexual feelings alive in the field, then his or her own, as well as the patient's, capacity to think about sensual/bodily/sexual feelings can develop in both patient and analyst. Of course, this sounds easy in the abstract, but is not so easy in the heat of the moment.

## Clinical Material: 'Pick-up' Sticks

'Frank', a sensitive 12-year-old boy with a 'cool', teenage demeanor, appeared at least two years older than his actual age. He was in analysis for depression following his father's death. His mother suffered a chronic depression and was further collapsed in relation to her husband's illness and death. Now, two years into the analysis, Frank's depression had diminished and an erotic transference developed, partly under the pressure of puberty and also in response to our having begun a fourth weekly session. Frank had agreed to a fourth weekly session because he could see that our work was helping him to use his mind more actively to sort out his own feelings from his mother's feelings. He had observed: "[W]hen my mother is depressed I feel like I can feel her feelings." His mother accepted my recommendation of a fourth session because she was concerned both about Frank's painful stutter and about some of Frank's 'risky' friends.[6]

Frank felt that I had a special interest in him as demonstrated by my wanting to see him so often. He at first complained that the fourth session was too much time and took away from other things. However, at one point I noted aloud that he seemed distant following my having been away. I commented: "It's easy to feel if someone is not there, that they don't care about you." He replied: "I know you care about me because of the fourth session." This was the end of the hour, and before he got up he touched my leg with one of the pick-up sticks we had been playing with and commented that my stockings were "shiny." I am reminded of Freud's (1915: 169) comment in 'Observations on transference love,' that the analyst "has evoked this love by instituting analytic treatment in order to cure the neurosis."

At times I noticed Frank looking at my breasts.[7] Another time he looked at my legs and asked: "Are they stockings?" I said: "Guys your age are often curious about girls' things, like stockings and underwear. Another thing about your age is that there are a lot of intense changes in one's body that can often feel hard to talk about." Frank replied with emotion: "I know what you mean. I'm beginning to have acne and other people my age aren't getting it yet."

In another session Frank touched my wedding ring and asked:

*F:*   What stone is it?
*A:*   You may be wondering not just what stone, but what the ring means.
*F:*   That you're married.
*A:*   Maybe, but then there's also what that means to you because you're pretty close to me.
*F:*   Have you seen the movie *When Harry Met Sally*? The man in the movie didn't notice the woman at first.
*A:*   You are noticing girls more in general but also noticing me in that way.

It was near the end of the session and Frank was tracing the veins in his forearm with his finger. I was struck by the change in his forearm over the last two years I had seen him – his forearm had changed from that of a boy to that of a man. At this moment I felt attracted to him in the same way as I might toward an adult, masculine man. At 12 he had already largely developed the body of a man. It has often been observed that it is a challenge for girls who menstruate early to integrate their experiences, having had less time for antecedent emotional and cognitive development. It is also true for boys who have the bodies of men without the same psychological development.

Frank hummed the 'Wedding March' under his breath another day, and more than once slipped and asked why we hadn't met on the fifth day, on which we did not have an appointment. I pointed out he might be wishing we met that day as well. I mentioned the possibility of a fifth session to his mother, who spoke of it to an uncle Frank was close to. Frank's mother and uncle seemed to have an underlying suspicion regarding my interest in Frank. Indeed, I had to struggle to sort out my own feelings of attraction to Frank to keep myself from withdrawing from him due to anxiety about my erotic countertransference.

The following interchange seems to capture the incestuous aspects of the transference, and the anxieties surrounding it:

*F:*   I was reading about a Japanese gangster who got shot nine times, shot through the mouth, tongue, teeth. With leprosy could you have a finger fall off?

*A:*    Where did you hear about that possibility?

*F:*    In history class. I think it could happen.

*A:*    It reminds me of an old wives' tale that if a guy masturbates enough his penis could fall off. It's not true, but I guess it comes from that part of a guy's body being really important to him [Frank nods] and worrying something could happen to it.

*F:*    In French tutorial today we were done with work, so we were just chilling, and somebody raised the story of a teacher who had sex with her 12-year-old student, and he got her pregnant. She was married and had three children. She went to jail, and when she got out, he got her pregnant again.

*A:*    What did you think about that story?

*F:*    It's weird, 24 years older is a little bit of a problem – she was 36. [Frank trails off.]

*A:*    Maybe you're uncomfortable talking about it, as I'm an older woman you're close to, and you're 12.

Frank was unable to say any more about this issue, but I felt that it crystallized the transference-countertransference situation. I said: "I don't think it was good what happened between the teacher and student, but I wouldn't want you to think such feelings are weird." I gulped internally as I linked this loaded story directly to our relationship. There had been many indicators of Frank's feelings, so it did not feel premature. I also felt confident that I was not being seductive, but was naming something implicit in order to make it more explicit.

There could be reasons to allow material to continue to evolve in derivative form, as well as times it could feel over-stimulating to make a direct link to the analytic couple. As I look back many years later, this comment has a feeling of rightness to me. The situation in the room was stimulating – a boy going through puberty and an older woman. I felt toward Frank as I might when attracted to a man, including some preoccupation with these feelings outside of sessions. Within the privacy of my sexual fantasy there were also elements of an older, more sexually experienced woman with a virile, but unexperienced young boy/man. I was also well aware that Frank was not actually a young man, but a boy. I believe that my ways of relating to him in the hours always kept this in mind, but that the transitions in him were stimulating to him and to me.

Soon after, Frank told me that his uncle asked: "Did your analyst propose yet?" Frank said: "It's weird you want me to come so much, since most people go once or twice a week." I said: "Sometimes people are uncomfortable with positive feelings, but I imagine you felt confused about whose ideas to be loyal to." Frank nodded. He seemed to register that sharing and understanding his loving and sexual feelings could be helpful to him. I think that my effort to bear with my erotic feelings toward Frank, despite these accusations and my own discomfort, helped Frank to tolerate and integrate his own sexual and romantic feelings more fully.

## Discussion

My comments to Frank were intended to have an open-ended "unsaturated" (Bion, 1962) quality, in order to allow Frank's feelings, thoughts and experiences to develop further. New bodily sensations and related emotions can feel like a taboo area to both patient and analyst. An analyst has to be willing to brave this territory if she expects her patient to be able to. While it is often useful to proceed in an unsaturated manner, it is especially true in relation to the physical changes of adolescence. The bodily changes and sensations of adolescence are so big that they can only be taken in gradually.

When helping an adolescent to name erotic feelings, we are also indirectly implying certain attitudes toward sexuality – that it's there, that sexuality is part of us, that even very intense feelings can be shared. When I look back at this material it seems right to me that I did not interpret Frank's story about the teacher in relation to incestuous feelings toward his mother (while of course there would be an element of truth to this). Such a genetic interpretation would have been avoidant of the erotic feelings in the room and could have signaled to Frank my unwillingness to be close to his feelings.

An analyst might not directly interpret derivative material in some situations. The "perverse" children described by Alvarez (2012: 122) might take such an interpretation in an addictive direction and be unable to use it to think. Sexually over-stimulated or abused adolescents might be better served by discussing sexuality in more derivative form, as they have too often been victim to sexuality crashing through. Over-concrete children, such as those on the Autism Spectrum, would be unlikely to use an explicit transference interpretation fluidly, rendering such comments useless or confusing. Also, a therapist must consider how much preparatory groundwork there is in a treatment that might allow intense feelings to be taken on with more confidence. Frank had already been in analysis for two years and we had weathered some other storms.

Of course, we must always observe reactions to what we have said and have an attitude of humility that while we may have intended a comment in one way, it may be experienced in another. It is my impression that interpreting this material to Frank more explicitly was useful. Leaving these feelings unnamed could imply that they were too catastrophic to identify. Instead, very loaded feelings were named and the boundaries and purposes of our work remained in place.

Retrospectively, the erotic transference-countertransference with Frank emerged at a specific time in the treatment and was more in the background subsequently. Shortly after my patient's erotic transference to me reached a height (now 13 years old), he started a romantic relationship with a girl his age. She was his girlfriend over the next two years. I was impressed with Frank's growing ability to talk directly with her about his feelings.

I believe that the erotic transference experienced with an emotionally available but safe object became a launching ground for Frank's own erotic life. I thought that his experience of having a single object who was paying attention to him, and to whom he was paying attention, allowed for a deepening of a capacity for intimacy. His mother's depression likely made "the potentiating capacity of eroticism" (Elise, 2017: 35) more important in the analytic relationship than it might have been had these feelings been more available in his family.

Adolescents frequently present with bravado, which masks their developmental unreadiness for some experiences. I believe that the period of erotic transference-countertransference allowed Frank a trying-on of feelings and fantasies, as well as some room to verbalize these experiences. Adolescent treatment often has this quality – a dress rehearsal[8] is allowed for issues that feel unsafe – either for reasons of conflict, or developmental unreadiness. Adolescents often experience first love with an unavailable object, but important growth is happening meanwhile.

My experience of Frank's erotic transference is much as Searles described in his 1958 paper 'Oedipal love in the countertransference.' That is, that the child accepts the unrealizability of his oedipal strivings not mainly through fear of and identification with the forbidding rival parent, but

> through the ego strengthening experience of finding that the beloved parent reciprocates his love – responds to him, that is, as being a worthwhile and lovable individual, as being indeed a conceivably desirable love partner – and renounces him only with an accompanying sense of loss on the parent's own part . . . This child emerges . . . with his ego strengthened out of the knowledge that his love, however unrealizable, is reciprocated.
>
> (Searles, 1958: 188)

Concomitantly, emotional dulling can occur if the "beloved parent had to repress his or her reciprocal desire for the child, chiefly through the mechanism of unconscious denial of the child's importance to the parent" (Searles, 1958: 189).

Davies, an American Relational analyst, suggests that erotic transference can be infantilized and seen only in pre-oedipal or oedipal dimensions. She suggests that as inhibitions or symptoms caused by infantile conflicts are understood, "the rich efflorescence, not the disappearance of passionate desire in the analytic relationship" often ensues. Within the "relatively safe confines of the analytic space . . . there is a freedom to experience those aspects of sexual desire and erotic fantasy that are part of emergent self-experiences" (1998: 752).

Davies relates a riveting moment from her own family life, which she felt informed her understanding of emergent adolescent sexuality. Davies and her husband were engrossed in conversation when their daughters (who had been playing dress-up) ran by. The 12-year-old

> had piled her long dark hair on top of her head and had put on a clingy black jersey, slit up the side. The outfit was completed with black fishnet stockings, patent-leather high heels and a red garter. I was astounded, but her father let slip an almost imperceptive but still subliminally audible gasp – a gasp heard loud and clear by his very vulnerable daughter woman and her then immobilized but horrified mother. In a series of microseconds, meaningful looks of danger and confusion ricocheted spitfire around this now palpable triangle, and my daughter, crying hysterically, ran from the room.
>
> (1998: 759)

Gathering himself, Davies' husband went to talk to his daughter. Later, equilibrium apparently restored, Davies asked what he had said to accomplish this:

> "I told her the truth," he said, "that I had never seen her looking so beautiful before . . . in such a grown-up way . . . that it had taken my breath away . . . that I liked it . . . but that it was something I was going to have to get used to." "Did she say anything?" I asked. "No," but she smiled the most beautiful smile." And then he smiled.
>
> (1998: 760)

Davies suggests that her husband's honest acknowledgment allows a "beginning recognition" of adolescent emergent sexual subjectivity and of the parental capacity to both recognize it and deal with his or her own response to it in a thoughtful manner. An adolescent can experience being the object of another's sexual response in a reasonably titrated manner when that response is both forthright and contained. I was struck by the pauses in the husband's speech, which Davies represented three times by ". . ." These pauses seem to me a helpful communication in addition to the words themselves. The pauses imply that one can stop to think when in the midst of tumultuous feelings.

The analyst of an adolescent must be able to withstand a series of anxieties in relation to sexuality – e.g., "Is what we're talking about too much?" "Is it too exciting?" "Is my interest too voyeuristic?" – in order to help the adolescent tolerate her or his own excitements and anxieties. This willingness to tread in an anxiety-provoking and taboo area can hopefully lend what I call an 'erotic sufficiency' to our work with adolescents. Dimen suggests: "[A]nalysts' ability to contain their own desire with self-awareness equates to parents' observance of the incest prohibition. Such self-conscious containment creates and protects a gap in which the patient's subjectivity can come into its own (Bernstein, 2006)" (2011: 59).

Lombardi (2017) comments: "[A]dolescence involves confrontation with a *choice* that becomes decisive for all subsequent development: this choice consists of either facing up to adolescent turbulence or mobilizing all possible strategies to avoid it" (2017: 113). This period of treatment felt turbulent to me as well as, I imagine, to Frank. While I do not feel I was at any point inappropriate or flirtatious in the sessions, outside of the hours I thought I must have been losing my mind to have strong feelings of attractions to a 12-year-old. In retrospect, I think that Frank and I were able to sustain turbulence without closing it down too quickly, yielding an 'erotic sufficiency.'

## Erotic Field

My work with Frank took place a decade and a half ago when I was still a candidate in child analysis. As I reflect on it now, I am struck that my experience with Frank was of a "bi-personal field" (Baranger & Baranger, 2008; Molinari, 2017), "analytic third" (Ogden, 1994), or "intermediate area of experience" (Winnicott, 1971), though the Freudian supervision I was in at the time did not employ this language. My experience was of a continuous exchange of emotional elements that through dreams and narratives (such as the 12-year-old impregnating his 36-year-old teacher) "find a way of expressing and narrating what is going on in the depths of the relational exchange" (Ferro, 1999: 158).

Shared meanings and feelings could be elaborated with Frank in a way that did not have to be too pinned down. Meanings could continually take shape from a shared (though not directly expressed on my part) experience of erotic and romantic longings. These longings could also come into contact with a reality of limits in the relationship and the allowance that these longings be transformed for other purposes, such as Frank's assumption of his romantic and erotic life. It is interesting that while coming from a Freudian view that emphasized the intra-psychic, my supervisor seemed entirely comfortable with this way of working.

The supervision[9] I was in was instrumental in helping me not to inhibit erotic feelings in my relationship with Frank. The use of a consultant may be particularly important in an erotic field to help (as Bion says) to think while feeling and feel while thinking. In the context of the above clinical moment I recall my supervisor saying that it was good that I liked males, implying that Frank did not have to be deprived of the subtle ways this would come across in my interactions with him. I am reminded of Elise's comment:

[W]hat of the analyst's libidinal investment in that unique patient, in that analysis. An analysis cannot rest on the patient's libidinal energies alone. We might think of erotic energy as circulating in multiple directions in the intersubjective field of an analysis – a libidinally alive matrix . . . A clinical situation of vibrancy can foster patients' increased libidinal investment in *themselves*.

(2017: 49)[10]

It is interesting to consider how the work with Frank might have been different with a heterosexual male analyst or a gay or lesbian analyst. It is important for all analysts to be fluid and imaginative in experiencing ourselves as male or female, father or mother, or in a homosexual or heterosexual role with a patient. Still, it seems to me there are times that the specific genders of the pair are important, and perhaps especially so at puberty. Some early adolescent girls relate to me as if I may be able to help figure out the mysteries that are befalling them – after all, I have gone through similar bodily changes. In the current clinical material, the constellation of a heterosexual boy in early adolescence and a heterosexual female analyst may have allowed a particularly intense version of feelings that surely would have also been present in some form with this patient and a different analyst.

The terms 'erotic transference' and 'erotic countertransference' seem to me too static to capture the fluidity, subtlety or complexity that is better conveyed in the dynamic concept of an 'erotic field.' Hartmann (2017), in a memorial paper for Muriel Dimen, highlights her complex use of field theory. He says: "[B]etter to speak to/in the erotic field than to codify it as the patient's 'erotic transference.' To reify the transference is to forget that 'recursively, to reflect on desire and to contain it, enhance each other' (Dimen, 2011, p. 59)" (Hartmann, 2017: 133).

When I think back to the period in my work with Frank when erotic feelings were in the forefront, it feels almost impossible to say 'whose feeling is it?' Frank experienced my recommendation of frequent sessions as a possible seduction. His looking at my body was stimulating to me. I think of the complexity of any single moment such as when Frank traced the veins on his forearm and I felt attracted to him as I might to an adult, masculine man. These were my feelings, located in me and unspoken. But Frank's subtle and un-self-conscious action might also represent a new sensuality and budding awareness of his body, which I was also reacting to.

At times there are feelings that might belong mainly to one member of the analytic couple. Frank felt frustrated that I did not let him in on my private life. But even such an experience (that was mainly his) includes a whole history of familial boundary experiences for both patient and analyst. Such personal experience of boundaries would become in some way part of the erotic field.

## Conclusion

Analytic work with adolescents brings to mind words like *visceral, intense, in motion* and *palpable*. At times adolescents have been considered poorly suited for analytic treatment[11] (A. Freud, 1958). The changing body of the adolescent patient presents particular challenges to containment and pressures toward enactment in the treatment of adolescents. Lombardi, commenting on Ferrari, notes: "[A] lack of experience with the adult world establishes the necessity for the adolescent to 'act in order to know' (Ferrari, 2004)" (2016: 4). When analysis can help an adolescent to understand and contain their bodily and familial changes, the bodily-based psychopathologies (eating disorders, cutting, substance abuse) which are characteristic disturbances of adolescence (Anderson, 2004; Brady, 2016) may be prevented or mitigated.

In the next chapter I will consider a different hot topic in analytic work with adolescents. There, I will relate the analytic psychotherapy of a gay teen struggling with his emerging sexuality in the context of internalized and external homophobia. My work with this boy also required me to grapple with my own internalization of homophobic aspects of psychoanalytic developmental theory.

As I complete this chapter, I think about its title. Is it 'entering' the erotic field with the adolescent patient or some other verb: what about 'surviving' or 'tolerating' or 'enjoying' or 'playing in' or 'braving?' As I mull over these verbs, they all have some element of truth, but 'braving' is perhaps the most fitting – and thus the title changes . . . I will end this chapter with Alvarez's reminder that:

> Sometimes the positive transference is harder to take and stay with than the negative; and when it is sexual, too, it demands much courage, honesty and respect from us in our countertransference responses.
>
> (2012: 129)

## Acknowledgment

At time of writing, this chapter was also set to appear as: Brady, M.T. (2018). Braving the erotic field in the treatment of adolescents. *Journal of Child Psychotherapy, 44*(2).

## Notes

1 A search of Pep-Web resulted in 1,785 references for *erotic transference*, 592 references for *erotic countertransference*, 15 references for *erotic transference, adolescence* and only three references for *erotic counter-transference, adolescence*. For a recent welcome exception to this neglect, see *Journal of Child Psychotherapy*, 2017, *43*(1), which is devoted to adolescent treatment, and "opens with three papers which tackle the real-ity of sexual and erotic transference, and the handling of this, within the psychotherapies of adolescent patients. As each author remarks, the litera-ture on the topic has historically been somewhat slender" (Stratton, K., & Russell, J., 2017).

2 For an exception to this generalization see Alvarez's description of "perverse sexuality" (2012: 122) in a seven-year-old child.

3 It would be interesting to study the responses of adolescents to the use of the couch. In my experience some adolescents find the use of the couch sexually stimulating and others find it a refuge that helps them to talk about sexual feelings without having to look at the analyst, or these may both be true at different times.

4 Person's (1985) paper on erotic transference in adults contends that male patients are more resistant to the awareness of the erotic transference and that female patients are more resistant to the resolution of the erotic transference in the cross-gendered treatments she studied. It would be interesting to study this question in adolescent treatments. In adolescence, particularly at puberty, the gender of the pair may matter more than at any other age.

5 In contrast to a classical view of countertransference as a hindrance, espoused by Reich (1951).

6 It is interesting to note the different but perhaps related issues that led this teen and his mother to accept a recommendation for more intensive work. Frank's acceptance of the recommendation followed his recognition of newfound vigor as he began to use his mind to separate himself from his mother's sunken depression. His mother's not-unrealistic concern that Frank would get in trouble with his risk-taking friends involved the dangers of separation.

7 Atkinson and Gabbard (1995) note that voyeuristic looking precedes genital sexuality in the ordinary sexual development of boys. Lena comments on a 16-year-old boy's gaze "to penetrate into my eyes or to stare at my body. I felt very uncomfortable, embarrassed, intruded upon, at times repulsed by him" (2016: 47). The intrusive quality of that boy's gaze was later understood as related to intrusion he had suffered. Frank's gaze seemed more as Atkinson and Gabbard describe.

8 See Laufer (1968, p. 115) about masturbation and masturbation fantasies in adolescence as "trial action" sometimes leading to developmental progression and sometimes to deadlock. My emphasis here is on the emergence of erotic feelings within the analytic work.

9  It is noteworthy that in the few articles I could find on working with the erotic transference with adolescents, supervision was frequently mentioned: e.g., Lena: "Supervision represented a vital 'third' that enabled me to think about the dangers of focusing only on the maternal and infantile aspects while avoiding talking about sexuality" (2016: 53).

10  Clearly Elise recognizes that "the analyst's creative energies are not to be a substitute for the absence of such energies in the patient; rather, they are best seen as an enlivening contribution to the analytic encounter, even if, paradoxically, they are used to narrate deadness and devitalization" (2017: 51).

11  Anna Freud (1958) thought that adolescents separating from their objects were not able to sufficiently "transfer" or attach to a new object, which made them difficult or impossible to treat. She felt that help might instead be aimed at their parents. Though many analysts did not share her view, it did seem to have a chilling effect on attitudes toward the intensive treatment of adolescents for some time. A panel discussion at the American Psychoanalytic Association on analysis of adolescents, summarized by Sklansky, concluded "few contemporary adolescent patients are analyzable . . . once in analysis a variety of parameters of technique far beyond those used in the classical analysis of adults are necessary" (1972: 134). The one dissenting panelist was Adatto, who commented that certain adolescents with "sufficient ego capacities and transference readiness can catapult an analysis into intensive productive work, rarely observed in adults" (1972: 138). More recent literature has emerged which differs from this concern regarding adolescent analyzability (Laufer, 1997; Paz & Olmoz de Paz, 1992).

## References

Alvarez, A. (2012). Types of sexual transference and countertransference in work with children and adolescents. In *The Thinking Heart: Three Levels of Psychoanalytic Therapy with Disturbed Children*. Hove and New York, NY: Routledge, pp. 116–129.

Anderson, R. (2004). Adolescence and the body ego: The re-encountering of primitive mental functioning in adolescent development. *Unpublished paper presented at the 16th Annual Melanie Klein Memorial Lectureship*, January 8, 2005, Los Angeles, CA.

Atkinson, S., & Gabbard, G. (1995). Erotic transference in the male adolescent–female analyst dyad. *Psychoanalytic Study of the Child, 50*: 171–186.

Baranger, M., & Baranger, W. (2008). The analytic situation as a dynamic field. *International Journal of Psychoanalysis, 89*: 795–826.

Bernstein, J. W. (2006), Love, desire, jouissance: Two out of three ain't bad. Psychoanalytic Dialogues, 16:711–724.

Bion, W.R. (1962). *Learning from Experience*. London: Heinemann.

Blos, Sr., P. (1967). The second individuation process of adolescence. *Psychoanalytic Study of the Child, 22*: 162–186.

Blum, H. (1973). The concept of the erotized transference. *Journal of the American Psychoanalytic Association, 21*: 61–76.

Brady, M.T. (2016). *The Body in Adolescence: Psychic Isolation and Physical Symptoms*. New York: Routledge.

Davies, J.M. (1998). Between the disclosure and foreclosure of erotic transference and countertransference: Can psychoanalysis find a place for adult sexuality? *Psychoanalytic Dialogues, 8*: 747–766.

Dimen, M. (2011). *Lapsus linguae*, or a slip of the tongue: A sexual boundary violation in an analytic treatment and its personal and theoretical aftermath. *Contemporary Psychoanalysis, 47*: 35–79.

Elise, D. (2017). Moving from within the maternal: the choreography of analytic eroticism. *Journal of the American Psychoanalytic Association, 65*(1): 33–60.

Ferrari, A.B. (2004). *From the Eclipse of the Body to the Dawn of Thought*. London: Free Association Books.

Ferro, A. (1999). *The Bi-Personal Field: Experiences in Child Analysis*. London: Routledge.

Freud, A. (1958). Adolescence. *Psychoanalytic Study of the Child, 13*: 55–278.

Freud, S. (1915). Observations on transference love. In J. Strachey (Ed. & Trans.), *The Standard Edition of the Complete Psychological Works of Sigmund Freud, Vol. 12*: 159–171. London: Hogarth Press.

Greenberg, J., & Mitchell, S. (1983). *Object Relations in Psychoanalytic Theory*. Cambridge, MA: Harvard University Press.

Hartmann. S. (2017). Muriel Dimen, field theorist. *Studies in Gender and Sexuality, 18*: 132–135.

Holtzman, D., & Kulish, N. (1997). *Nevermore: The Hymen and the Loss of Virginity*. Northvale, NJ: Jason Aronson.

Jackson, E. (2017). Too close for comfort: The challenges of engaging with sexuality in work with adolescents. *Journal of Child Psychotherapy, 43*(1): 6–22.

Kristeva, J. (2014). Reliance, or maternal eroticism. *Journal of the American Psychoanalytic Association, 62*: 69–85.

Kulish, N. (1998). First loves and prime adventures: Adolescent expressions in adult analyses. *Psychoanalytic Quarterly, 67*(4): 539–565.

Langs, R. (1981). *The Therapeutic Experience and its Setting*. New York, NY: Jason Aronson.

Laufer, M. (1968). The body image, the function of masturbation, and adolescence: Problems of the ownership of the body. *Psychoanalytic Study of the Child, 23*: 114–137.

Laufer, M. (1997). Developmental breakdown in adolescence: Problems of understanding and helping. In M. Laufer (Ed.), *Adolescent Breakdown and Beyond*. Madison, IN: Indiana University Press.

Lena, F.E. (2017). Working with and 'seeing through': Sexual transference in the psychotherapy of an adolescent boy. *Journal of Child Psychotherapy, 43*(1): 40–54.

Little, M. (1951). Counter-transference and the patient's response to it. *International Journal of Psychoanalysis, 32*: 32–40.

Lombardi, R. (2016). Entering one's own life as a goal of clinical analysis. *Unpublished paper presented at the Scientific Meeting,* November 14, San Francisco Center for Psychoanalysis, San Francisco, CA.

Lombardi, R. (2017). Body and mind in adolescence. In *Body-Mind Dissociation in Psychoanalysis: Developments after Bion.* Abingdon and New York: Routledge, pp. 110–127.

Molinari, E. (2017). *Field Theory in Child and Adolescent Psychoanalysis: Understanding and Reacting to Unexpected Developments.* Abingdon and New York: Routledge.

Ogden, T.H. (1994). The analytic third: Working with intersubjective clinical facts. *International Journal of Psychoanalysis, 75*: 3–19.

Ogden, T.H. (1995). Analyzing forms of aliveness and deadness of the transference-countertransference. *International Journal of Psychoanalysis, 76*: 695–709.

Ogden, T.H. (1997). *Reverie and Interpretation.* Northvale, NJ: Jason Aronson.

Paton, I. (2017). Within or without: Negotiating psychic space with an adolescent at risk of developing a narcissistic personality structure. *Journal of Child Psychotherapy, 43*(1): 23–39.

Paz, C., & Olmoz de Paz, T. (1992). Adolescence and borderline pathology: Characteristics of the relevant psychoanalytic process. *International Journal of Psychoanalysis, 73*(4): 739–755.

Person, E. (1985). The erotic transference in women and in men: Differences and consequences. *Journal of the American Academy of Psychoanalysis and Psychiatry, 13*: 159–180.

Racker, H. (1953). A contribution to the problem of counter-transference. *International Journal of Psychoanalysis, 34*: 313–324.

Racker, H. (1957). The meanings and uses of countertransference. *Psychoanalytic Quarterly, 41*: 303–357.

Reich, A. (1951). On countertransference. *International Journal of Psychoanalysis, 32*: 25–31.

Samuels, A. (2000). The erotic leader. *Psychoanalytic Dialogues, 10*: 277–280.

Searles, H. (1958). Oedipal love in the countertransference. *International Journal of Psychoanalysis, 40*: 180–190.

Sklansky, M. (1972). Indications and contraindications for the psychoanalysis of the adolescent. *Journal of the American Psychoanalytic Association, 20*(1): 134–144.

Stratton, K., & Russell, J. (2017). Editorial. *Journal of Child Psychotherapy*, *43*(1): 1–5.

Winnicott, D.W. (1949). Hate in the countertransference. *International Journal of Psychoanalysis*, *30*: 69–74.

Winnicott, D.W. (1971). *Playing and Reality*. London: Tavistock.

# Chapter 2

# "Sometimes we are prejudiced against ourselves"

## Internalized and external homophobia in the treatment of an adolescent boy

This chapter considers the painful experiences of external and internal homophobia for an adolescent boy and his poignant use of the analytic setting to begin to name and claim his sexuality. I will also discuss aspects of my experience with this boy in relation to the impact of homophobia within psychoanalytic developmental theories. The historical pathologizing of homosexuality within developmental theories and the nascent state of psychoanalytic views of healthy homosexual development requires analytic clinicians to consider our internalization of homophobia and its potential effects on our patients. Paradoxically, my concern for the harm caused to this boy by homophobic attitudes made it harder to consider divergent or contradictory aspects of his sexuality.

When harm has been done to a child by some form of prejudice, it can evoke a protective reaction on the part of an analyst. However, this protectiveness toward a child stands in tension with any patient's need to be seen as complex and sometimes contradictory.

A serious consideration of normal homosexual development began only in the last 25 years.

> Much has been written about 'homosexuality' – or, to be precise, about its causes and cures – but until recently there has been almost no attention given by psychoanalysts to the experience of growing up gay and to the normative life courses of gay men and women.
>
> (Roughton, 2002: 735)[1]

This chapter is one of an increasing number of efforts to redress that gap (e.g., Corbett, 1996; Friedman & Downey, 2002; Hegna, 2007; Isay, 1989; Lingiardi, 2001). The paralysis of thought regarding homosexual development short-changes us all. My patient's increasing elaboration of a gay identity is part of the excitement of adolescent developments that I would like to convey in this chapter. It was less than two decades ago that the American Psychoanalytic Association adopted its 'Position Statement on the Treatment of Homosexual Patients' asserting that:

> (1) Same-gender sexual orientation cannot be assumed to represent a deficit in personality development or the expression of psycho-pathology. (2) As with any societal prejudice, anti-homosexual bias negatively affects mental health, contributing to an enduring sense of stigma and pervasive self-criticism in people of same-gender sexual orientation through the internalization of such preju-dice. (3) As in all psychoanalytic treatments, the goal of analysis with homosexual patients is understanding. Psychoanalytic technique does not encompass purposeful efforts to 'convert' or 'repair' an individual's sexual orientation. Such directed efforts are against fun-damental principles of psychoanalytic treatment and often result in substantial psychological pain by reinforcing damaging internalized homophobic attitudes.
>
> (1999)

The experience of homophobia is acutely painful – as is any rejection we suffer on the basis of something intrinsic to us, such as sexual orientation, race, religion or gender. The clinical material I will offer is intended as one lens through which we may consider the effects of homophobia, their internalization, how they become entangled with intrapsychic processes, and the protective but harmful measures used to handle rejection (in this boy, school avoidance and narcissistic defenses). These defensive forma-tions became understandable in light of the homophobia this boy suffered and internalized, as well as the lack of sufficient concern in his environ-ment for his needs. Without an appreciation of the effects of homophobia, a boy like this could easily be seen as more disturbed than he really was. In Straker's words:

> Psychoanalysis . . . needs to extend itself beyond an analysis of the wishes and passions themselves, to an understanding of how . . . we come to be gripped in the coils of toxic social histories in order to make our unthinking performativity of these histories more thinkable.
>
> (2006: 740)

## Internalized Homophobia

Divergent emphases have emerged in the psychoanalytic literature on internalized homophobia. Moss, in an article on internalized homophobia in men, argues "the most powerful clinical use of the term depends upon its applicability to any man [or presumably woman], without limitation to those whose primary object choice is homosexual" (2002: 21). He describes internalized homophobia in men as a movement from a personal subjective experience of homosexual impulses, which, if threatening, is defended against by a movement toward identifying with "masculine" group hatred toward homosexuality. He notes that the conventional usage of the term "internalized homophobia"

> aims to describe and to partially account for a sexual identity charac-terized by persistent, structured negative feelings, particularly shame and self-loathing. Implicit . . . is the idea that such feelings represent the dynamic outcome of an internalization of the dominant culture's attitude toward homosexuality.
>
> (2002: 22)

Moss recognizes that the advantage of this definition is that gays and les-bians bear the brunt of the pain from homophobia and that this definition recognizes the difference between victims and perpetrators. He argues, however, that internalized homophobia is a symptom also applicable to heterosexual identified patients, albeit of less virulence than that for gay patients. Roughton, in a response to Moss, contends that "internalized homophobia is . . . not just about sex, but about self-concept . . . What is needed therapeutically is not to discover what the 'symptom' substitutes for, but to alter one's basic concept of self" (Roughton, 2002, quoted in Moss, 2002).

Moss emphasizes internalized homophobia as a symptom related to renouncing threatening sexual impulses, whereas Roughton (following Malyon, 1982) emphasizes self-concept. Both levels of thought seem clinically and theoretically useful, although Roughton's assertion of inter-nalized homophobia as a term primarily applicable to homosexuals seems compelling to me. Although it is undoubtedly true that heterosexuals can be prejudiced against their homosexual inclinations, that pain seems of a different order than for people whose basic sense of self is deeply con-nected to their homosexuality, both at the levels of sexuality and identity.

Nonetheless, I find Moss's reminder that the concept of internalized homophobia relates not only to relatively accessible dimensions of experience but also to profoundly unconscious dynamics essential. He points to the complex manner in which the internalization of social, cultural and familial rejections combines with intrapsychic issues:

> Internalized homophobia is a symptomatic structure. Conceptually it is best thought of as a multilevel phenomenon. At a minimum it refers both to the widespread internalization of the dominant culture's interdiction against homosexuality and to a particular individual's defensive and possibly idiosyncratic employment of the interdiction.
>
> (2002: 49)

That is, the internalization of prejudice meets the complexities of psychic reality and developmental processes, intermingling into complex states of shame and superego judgment. Harris pithily expresses it as follows: "Homophobia, like many aspects of ideology, is both in us and we are in it" (1996: 363).

## Adolescence

Adolescence is the phase of all phases in which the struggle with both sexuality and identity is engaged, and the result is either development or various forms of defendedness (or even collapse). Adolescents come up against societal and familial expectations and prejudices, which interact with their intrapsychically determined wishes, fears, defenses and developing identities. Typical fears and confusions can be far more likely to rigidify into internalized homophobia if an adolescent does not have an environment that facilitates and contains his or her sexuality.

Winnicott (1965) calls our attention to the critical role of cultural experience and the family environment on the developing personality (in addition to intrapsychic factors). He sees the "maturational processes" only developing insofar as there is a "facilitating environment." Winnicott describes the characteristic nature of the maturational process as the drive toward integration. In adolescence, this could be an increasingly integrated sense of bodily experience, object relations and self-concept. Ideally, an adolescent can integrate a sense of what is most compelling, for instance, in terms of sexual orientation, without having to eschew divergent impulses and inclinations as also part of the self.

As analysts of adolescents we have the dual tasks of working with parents to help them engage with the needs of their child, and of providing a facilitating environment within the treatment for the adolescent's developing sexuality. Winnicott (1961) sees the analyst as, ideally, similar to a competent mother who allows her child to develop in her or his own fashion without a preconceived path. This enables the patient free play with her or his own thoughts and feelings. Winnicott reminds us that adults must not abdicate, or adolescence cannot really occur. My experience with the boy I will discuss echoes Winnicott's observation that "we may surely think of the strivings of adolescents to find themselves and to determine their own destiny as the most exciting thing that we can see in life around us" (1961: 146–147).

Mid-adolescence (the developmental stage of the boy I will present) is characterized "by the emergence of the adolescent's gendered and sexual self from the family into the social world. Middle adolescents move out from their families into the world of their peers to explore how their more definitively shaped bodies work" (Levy-Warren, 1996: 70). External and internalized homophobia can clearly interfere with the tasks of mid-adolescence. My patient's withdrawal would have delayed the important experimentation with internal and external experiences that takes place through deepening friendships and first romances. Adolescents try things on, and in doing so they see what fits. Internalized homophobia stunts the free play of fantasy and waylays trial actions.

Malyon suggests that the most likely developmental pathway for adolescent males (his research sample was solely gay males) "is an interruption (sometimes temporary, but often lasting a decade or more) of the process of identity formation" (1982: 61). He views peer group norms and prevailing social attitudes as incompatible with homosexual identity formation, resulting in a "bi-phasic process for most gay males" (62), with the final consolidation of sexual identity not occurring until the time of coming out. He contends that coming out allows the individual to renegotiate internalized homophobia and partially repair ego and identity formation.

Phillips (2001, 2002) describes a common finding that during mid-adolescence, gay males were "falling in love with and pining away for heterosexual adolescent boys" (2002: 131). He sees this as a progressive effort on the part of the homosexual boy to rework aspects of his oedipal attraction and rejection from his father. He cites Isay's (1989) conceptualization of a developmental pathway for gay men that entails homoerotic fantasies from at least age 4 or 5, analogous to oedipal struggles in hetero-sexual boys, except with the father as the object of desire.

I would underline Isay's (1989) emphasis on the importance of gay peer relations, at any stage, but especially in mid-adolescence. How could an adolescent conceive of the possibilities of what it means to be gay unless he or she has peer relationships in which to experiment?[2] Isay expresses concern that "on the whole, analytically oriented psychotherapists have little understanding of the importance of these attachments for the enhancement of self-esteem" (1989: 62). Peer relationships also allow teens a valuable route to developing their own identities: "[S]ocial stigmatization is particu-larly damaging to the adolescent and young adult because of the importance of peer acceptance in the task of separation from parents" (66). I will explore these issues through the experience of my patient, 'Mario'.

## Mario

Mario is a 14-year-old Italian American boy whom I've treated in twice-weekly psychotherapy. His father is a chemist and his mother is a homemaker. He has two brothers, who are three and five years older than he is. His parents sought therapy for Mario because his school-work deteriorated and he became school-avoidant. His parents said there had been a recent painful incident in which the father of Mario's best friend did not want his son to see Mario because he thought Mario was gay. Mario's parents said they did wonder if their son was gay, and that they would want him to know they would love him if he were. There seemed to be a serious lack of communication in the family, because they had not broached the issue at all, despite this painful incident. The parents described Mario as a quirky boy who likes modern dance and sometimes wears makeup. They described him as emotionally closer to his mother than to his father.

### First meeting

Mario is a slight boy. At our first meeting he was dressed in tight jeans with a fringed headband tied around his head. He seemed pretentious and defensive at first, expressing an intellectual interest in psychoanalysis. At times, his thinking seemed close to psychotic. For instance, in this first session he said:

*M:*   My way of thinking is that if you really believe something then it's true. Like if I believe that chair is blue, then it would be blue. But I don't quite believe it is, so it isn't. The most extreme example is something I was reading about someone who turned into a were-wolf. He believed he was a werewolf, so he was. He was hairy and had big teeth.

*A:*   You're talking about complicated things, and maybe two different ideas. One is that you can change reality with your mind, and another might have something to do with perception – that if this boy felt like a werewolf because of his hairiness and teeth, he might start thinking he actually was a werewolf.

*M:*   Yes, or like the placebo effect that some doctor gives someone a pill and their disease gets better even though there was nothing in the pill.

*A:*   I was thinking it might feel scary coming to a doctor like me – what effects I might have on you. I think of this as our thinking about things together. That you know a lot about yourself, I am getting to know you and we'll think together.

*M:*   I like the sound of that.

My initial impression was that the sexual changes of adolescence (as rep-resented by the werewolf) were very frightening to Mario, and that his anxiety at beginning treatment was intense. When these anxieties were commented on, he began to be able to speak in a more natural way about his problems. Later in this session, Mario said: "I have a Berlin Wall with people and I know it's going to come down sometime – fall down or get pushed down. But I don't know whether that's a good or a bad thing. When I see rays coming through they're red. Like people I don't like and a sinister world." I thought that he had a fear of something psychotic[3] breaking through, or perhaps was so frightened of his emerging sexuality that he experienced this natural development as potentially catastrophic.

## Homosexuality: coming out in therapy and elsewhere

Mario did not immediately introduce the issue of his sexual orientation, but because of the difficulties being open at home, I raised the issue in the second session. I said I knew there had been a painful incident with a friend who had not been allowed to see him as his father thought Mario was gay. I said that I wondered whether such things were difficult to talk about in his family, and that I wanted him to know it was important for him to be able to figure out who he was sexually and in other ways and to let me know if he had any worries about my reactions. He quickly indicated that he thought of himself as gay. I said that part of his coming to treatment might have to do with being able to find a way to talk with his family about this issue. He agreed, but said he knew he had other problems as well. Aside from his fears about being accepted as a gay boy, the other issues apparent from the beginning were social problems and a range of fears and phobias, including a horror of meat, which he called "flesh."[4] Not being allowed to spend time with his best friend because of his perceived homosexuality was acutely painful. Mario also told me of numerous hurtful, if less extreme, incidents – such as his brother saying an openly gay professor was "disgusting."

Soon after telling me he was gay, Mario also told his mother. He and his father did not talk about it directly. I encouraged his father to speak with Mario after Mario had told his mother, as otherwise it might seem that there was something too difficult to speak of. Father sent Mario a letter saying he accepted him as he was, but, of course, the distance involved in not being able to talk directly still came across. A month or so later Mario came out at his school. He was 13, in eighth grade at a progressive, private school, and his coming out was generally viewed by peers and teachers as courageous.[5] I thought this was an important step in claiming his identity. His school avoidance completely ceased. Mario said: "I feel quite differently about school now that I am able to talk about things." The presenting symptom of his school avoidance and academic decline abated after coming out in therapy and elsewhere, and these symptoms have not recurred.

Although I explicitly interpreted the probable link between Mario's school avoidance and the painful rejection he had suffered, it seemed to me that Mario's resumption of school attendance had more to do with his experience of finding a voice in therapy. Thus, he could go to school if he felt he could meet potential experiences of rejection with his own voice and perceptions. This made him feel less helpless in the face of prejudice.

### Narcissistic defenses and beginning intimacy

At times, Mario related to me in a rather self-important manner, as if he were a star and I his audience. His second regular weekly session had been disrupted by preparation for a dance performance. I think his not having a steady second time with me made him feel less accepted and secure and hence more reliant on rigid pseudo-adult, dramatic modes. Likewise, he was on the verge of finishing eighth grade and leaving the school he had attended for the past nine years. I continued to have the sense of Mario's performing and relying on narcissistic defenses until we were finally able to secure the second session. This required significant work with his parents. Soon after this was accomplished he began to relate more consistently in a manner that felt intimate, and to be able to sustain vulnerability and some pain.

Mario experienced the consolidated schedule as my taking his problems seriously, and then he could allow them into the room. In addition, knowing that he was not welcome by people who were homophobic made his being welcomed by me particularly important. His brittle, pseudo-adult presentation started to soften.

As Mario approached starting at his new high school, his anxieties about being accepted mounted. He particularly feared being treated as a stereotype instead of a real person in relation to being gay. As his anxiety was peaking at the beginning of the high school term, his mother expressed concern that the second session each week was too expensive, putting our schedule in question just as he most needed a firm container for his anxieties. In this context, he forgot to attend a session just before starting high school. I found his explanation for missing the session confusing and I was unsure of what had happened: whether either he or his mother had lied to me. He also related a story of a boy who had acted as if he liked Mario and instead went out with a girl. I said, "People tell me things in different ways – sometimes with words, for instance that something hurts, and other times they show me. On Monday, I was left alone, not knowing what was going on. I think it might have been a way of showing me how confusing it is for you to have someone say they like you and then to change their mind without any explanation."

Mario went on to talk about a number of guys he felt interested in or dropped by. His hurt at being turned down seemed magnified by his feelings about his homosexuality. He told me about a movie he had seen about eating disorders within the gay community and said: "Sometimes we are prejudiced against ourselves. I'm not prejudiced against others who are gay, but sometimes with myself." He felt intense anxiety in reaction to the combination of a new high school, his mother's disruption of the security of the therapy schedule, and his fears of being rejected for his homosexuality.

### Rejection by father

An important ongoing issue is Mario's feeling of rejection by his father. Although the father states that he accepts Mario's sexuality, he rarely spends time with Mario. The father is closer to Mario's older brothers, who are evidently heterosexual. Mario's father expresses considerable unhappiness at paying for Mario's therapy (which has become quite important to Mario), but does not balk at paying for expensive cars and trips for the older brothers. Mario feels that financial restrictions apply only to him in the family. This tacit rejection by his father leaves Mario feeling besieged – who he is and what he wants are not actively supported in the family. This rejection causes Mario to defend himself by acting as if he knows everything already and doesn't struggle with uncertainties and fears. At this point in the therapy I can comment on this defensive manner, and Mario is able to shift to describing his emerging sexual feelings more openly. Parenthetically, in these discussions, it is important to model that sexuality can be talked about openly. Although this is true in any therapy, it may be particularly true in treating gay adolescents who fear their sexuality will be frowned on.

### Social and romantic issues

As Mario navigated high school, he continued to be open about his sexuality, but this was not easy at times. He told me:

M: I don't like it when people make assumptions about who I am because I'm gay. I met this girl in my class at school. She and I were e-mailing and at some point I said I was gay, and she stepped way back and said: "I knew a gay person once."

A: I can see why it would feel bad to be treated as some very different kind of person, and especially when you're starting a new school.

M: Yes, and at my old school there were gay teachers. I had another kid I just met act like if you're gay you're immediately sexual, like you'd be immediately making out with someone.

A: You want people to get to know you in a more individual way, including me.

Mario went on to describe stereotypes he contends with in gay friends as well. He told a gay male friend about a straight male friend he valued and the gay friend responded: "Gay guys don't have straight friends, it doesn't work that way." I emphasized that although his sexual orientation was an important part of him, it was one of many parts of him. I said that he might be concerned about what stereotypes he or I might have about him.

Mario has also experienced homophobia in larger cultural arenas. He campaigned against Proposition 8,[6] and felt crushed when the ban on gay marriage in California passed. It was painful for Mario to be confronted with the fact that at that point the majority of Californians opposed gay marriage and, by extension, his hopes to be accepted on an equal footing in a gay relationship.

Mario has expressed fears regarding HIV. These fears seem part of a larger anxiety that he will not be looked after and prized as a gay boy – that others won't help to keep him safe. As I pointed out his fears that others and I won't look out for him, he has further softened and increasingly relates in a more intimate, serious manner. Although he has felt the rejection related to his homosexuality to be an extra burden to carry, I think at times he is able to feel I might help him with this challenge and work to keep him safe.[7]

In this year since he has come out, romantic relationships with other boys have also been complicated. He has had several romantic beginnings with boys, which have foundered because the other boys are still in the process of defining their sexual identities and are not ready to be seen publicly as gay. Although it is understandable that these other boys need time to come to terms with their sexuality and face the potential challenges of coming out in a homophobic society, this has added a level of frustration for Mario.

An important part of growing comfortable with one's sexuality in adolescence is to be able to experiment with it. This involves more than sexual acts. It pertains to all the wonderful and impossible aspects of teenage love. Mario has most recently been involved with a boy who is affectionate with him in private, but will not acknowledge him elsewhere. The other boy seems to be in a state of flux, saying that he is attracted to Mario but does not otherwise consider himself to be gay. Although the other boy's struggle is understandable, such experiences add frustration to Mario's natural and healthy wish to express his affection. Experimentation can be more difficult for gay teens than for their heterosexual counterparts, both because the majority of their peers will be heterosexual and also because potentially gay peers may be out of step in terms of their own coming-out process.

Mario has increasingly been able to use his therapy to move in the direction of having a "theory of mind" (Fonagy, Gergely, Jurist, & Target, 2002), i.e., an awareness of his own mental states that contributes to understanding the mental states of others. Other boys' romantic withdrawals from him have been hurtful, but he has been able to use his own experience of internalized homophobia to understand others' struggles with it. This has helped him to have a perspective that protects him from internalizing overwhelming feelings of rejection.

## Some Thoughts from a Heterosexual Analyst Treating a Probably Homosexual Boy

My training as a child analyst from 1999–2003 reflected the prevailing view of homosexuality and (especially) atypical gender identity within psychoanalytic developmental theory as developmental pathologies.[8] I was skeptical of those positions at the time and have increasingly come to reject these prejudices as preconceived orthodoxies and essentially anti-analytic. Thus, in treating gay adolescents I felt concerned regarding value judgments contained in developmental "normativities" (Corbett, 2001). I agree with Harris' view that analytic approaches to developmental theory and gender theory are "riddled with problems of power ideology, values and ethics" (quoted in Reis, 2003: 297).

One such normativity is the expectation that adolescents take up their 'proper' gender identity as well as 'sex-appropriate drive' and eschew gender variance. I could cite numerous examples in the developmental literature of a seemingly automatic pathologizing of homosexuality or nontraditional gender presentation. For instance, Harley states:

> I endeavor, then, to apply infinite care, in the analysis of passive homosexual problems, to respect openly the boy's attempts at active masculine behavior . . . If he gives danger signals of regressing to the point of surrender to his passivity, I try to counterbalance this by emphasizing the other side.

> (1970: 117)

Likewise, Blos, in his classic work *On Adolescence*, posits:

> Heterosexual object finding, made possible by the abandonment of the narcissistic and bisexual positions of early adolescence, characterizes the psychological development of adolescence proper. More precisely, we should speak of a gradual affirmation of the sex-appropriate drive moving into ascendancy and bringing increasingly conflictual anxiety to bear on the ego.
>
> (1962: 87)

Conversely, Blos writes:

> In the girl, two preconditions favor homosexual object choice. One is penis envy, which is overcompensated by contempt for the male; in these cases the girl herself acts like a boy in relation to other girls. The second precondition is an early fixation on the mother; in these cases the girl acts like a dependent child, slavishly obedient and trusting . . . In the boy, three preconditions favor the channeling of genital sexuality into a homosexual object choice during puberty. One is a fear of the vagina as a devouring castrating organ; we recognize in this unconscious concept a derivative of projected oral sadism. The second precondition resides in the boy's identification with the mother, a condition that is particularly apt to occur when the mother was inconsistent and frustrating while the father was either maternal or rejecting. A third precondition stems from the Oedipus complex which assumes the form of an inhibition or restriction summarily equating all females with mother and declaring introitus to be a father's prerogative.
>
> (1962: 105)

More recently, Tyson and Tyson note that in early adolescence a best friend relationship

> may initially provide an opportunity for both girls to elaborate fantasies about heterosexual escapades, [but] the dyadic oneness may lead to homosexual longings and experimentation. If so, this relationship may become so intense and gratifying that movement to a heterosexual position is delayed or thwarted altogether.
>
> (1990: 275)[9]

Across the ocean, Klein saw this issue similarly: "[W]hat has to be done during puberty is to organize the incoherent partial sexual instincts of the child towards procreative functions" (1922: 56).

Needless to say, all of these theorists have made major contributions to the understanding of adolescence. But what I object most to in these descriptions is the absence of any hint of consideration of a healthy homo-sexual development or non-pathological meanings to same-sex love. Homosexuality is seen as a regressive developmental arrest.[10] These views, it seems to me, run the risk of inflicting implicit moralizing, patronizing and unquestioning adherence to conventional value systems on our patients.

In a critique of this normativity, Corbett has discussed a complex mixture of feminine and masculine identifications in some boys who become homosexual. He notes: "The conflating of conformity with health has perhaps nowhere been more evident than in developmental theories of gender" (1996: 440). Indeed, I felt the problematic develop-mental literature on homosexuality as a ghost lurking in my treatment of Mario. Conversely, Freud's (1905) radical notion of psychic bisexuality, both in terms of identifications and object choice, remained a touchstone throughout this treatment.[11]

My concern regarding a stereotypic valuation for Mario of the 'proper' gender identity and devaluation of gender variance led to some hesitance in my exploration of aspects of his masculinity. During the last year, Mario has been dressing in a less flamboyant and somewhat more masculine style. I found myself hesitating to mention this change because of the possibility of implying that his increasing masculinity is what I would value most in him. But, of course, an overly cautious approach also has its costs in a free consideration of possibilities. I finally mentioned my observation of his change in dress. I said that I could appreciate that his earlier 'creative' dress had elements of freedom and experimentation to it, but that there might also be something signifi-cant to his increasing masculinity. His association was to a movie por-traying a heterosexual couple who returned to their favorite spot over and over. We understood this association as implying a sense that he experienced our sessions as 'dates' with important feelings of intimacy between us as a heterosexual couple. Finally, he also added that the boy he was getting increasingly intimate with was very masculine – seeming to imply that his object love involved a piece of seeking a masculinity he could internalize.[12] I relate this conversation not to settle the question, but to convey Mario's ease at considering multiple vertices. It increased my confidence that we could consider divergent aspects of his self with a sense of openness regarding their meaning or priority.

I also felt some conflict at times between a serious consideration of the effects of his experiences of homophobia, and considering possible meanings of Mario's gender identity or sexuality. Early in the treatment I was struck – and somewhat put off – by the flamboyance of Mario's dress (or, it might be more accurate to say, costumes). I felt jarred by his exaggerated presentation but also interested in remaining open in order to understand its meanings. For instance, Mario's father would complain of Mario's wearing spandex shorts, or going out in dramatic outfits including capes. Over time, I came to feel that Mario's exaggerated dress was related to feeling unseen and interpreted it as a fear that I would only be interested in his surface. Eventually, this exaggerated dress subsided, as I mentioned above. I have also considered the possibility that Mario's feminine dress might be provocative in relation to his father – with both meanings of the word 'provocative'. Clearly, Mario's father was put off by his dress, as I was. This could have an element of negative identification for Mario, i.e., "If you reject me for not being masculine I may as well go all the way with it." It could also be more simply a bid for his father's attention in the manner of a desirable female. Most recently, Mario has noticed that although he has felt rejected by his father, he has also avoided intimacy with his father when it is offered. In that sense, his dressing in a way that alienated his father (and me in the countertransference) was an unconscious effort to prevent intimacy. I also considered whether my unease with Mario's dress was related to his nontraditional gender presentation, and I think there is some truth to this. But I also have had a similar reaction to girls who arrive at my office dressed like Britney Spears. Although I feel sympathetic to the wish for a costume (and for the trying-on of identities), this sort of presentation can also feel unintegrated in contrast to an individuality of dress that feels more playful. At other times, I felt charmed by Mario's idiosyncratic and creative style.

My point is that the reality of homophobia has at times made me cautious about inferring complex meanings to Mario's sexuality. I believe, however, that this does Mario no favors. All of our sexualities are a multiply determined brew. It should not minimize the recognition of the hurt Mario has suffered through homophobia to view him, as any other patient, with full complexity and richness. An overly fearful attitude on my part due to the wish not to replicate homophobic attitudes could interfere with a full and free examination of sexuality.

I presented the clinical material related here at a panel of the International Psychoanalytic Association in 2009.[13] The discussant commented that I had foreclosed too quickly that the boy was homosexual and that Mario's "coming out has the structure of an acting out behavior, where the concerns that could have unfolded, formulated and contained in the frame of the transference, are evacuated or 'resolved' by means of an action on his environment" (Barredo, 2009). It is possible that either my own or Mario's anxieties about his sexuality could lead some questions to be avoided and instead translated into actions. However, I also feel it unlikely that a similar issue would have been raised in the presentation of a heterosexual adolescent. Could this be the quiet working of a heteronormative theory?[14] All of our sexualities are too complex to reduce to one-word descriptions such as 'heterosexual' or 'homosexual.' In that sense, such words are always oversimplifications. My concern, however, is that a probably gay adolescent's developing sense of sexuality could be treated with skepticism, and as a pathological structure.

Moreover, with adolescents, 'acting out' must be thought about differently than with adults. It is part of the challenge of working with adolescents to struggle with the mixtures of progressive and regressive meanings in their actions. For instance, even a destructive action such as drug abuse can, in part, be an effort at separation and new trial identifications, which are aspects of adolescent development. It is part of the challenge for analysts who treat adolescents to hear the multiple meanings of such actions. It is true that this boy came out without having carefully thought about the potential meanings ahead of time. I would say, however, that this is an important way that adolescents think – they try things on and see how they fit. I believe that Mario 'tried on' coming out with me and had some experience of applying the word 'gay' out loud to himself – and it fit. He also came to find that there were some ways the word did not fit – e.g., he expresses dislike at the substance abuse and promiscuity he sees as too prevalent in the gay community, and, as mentioned above, he experiences aspects of heterosexual love in our relationship. In addition, his claiming a voice in coming out – which seems to me a crucial part of claiming himself – e.g., the definitions and self-understandings can be elaborated, now that he feels a right to his own view of himself.

## Conclusion

Psychoanalysis offers a special opportunity for patients to distinguish between fantasy and reality and to evaluate the impact of societal stereotypes (group fantasies) on the internal world. For instance, Moss (1997) described the way in which HIV/AIDS could be used within a homophobic framework as a "natural" proof of homophobia. Such hateful and horrific ideas are potentially internalized by gay adolescents and entwined with intrapsychic processes. However,

> the psychoanalytic clinical literature, in addressing the upsurge in both the realistic and the fantasized dangers surrounding homoerotics, has maintained a steady, disinterested course . . . our recent literature on the points of convergence of HIV and homosexuality has remained essentially silent on the homophobias per se. (By 'our' I mean the English-language literature appearing in the *International Journal of Psycho-Analysis*, the *International Review of Psychoanalysis, Psychoanalytic Quarterly*, this journal [*Journal of the American Psychoanalytic Association*]).
>
> (Moss, 1997: 206)[15]

Moss comments further that

> we do not see what theory has not paved the path for us to see. For the most part, our clinical education, our received theories, have left us much less prepared, with either homosexual patients or with women to see, to theorize, to work and write clinically, on what may well seem to us the marginal problems of misogyny and homophobia.
>
> (1997: 206)

I have discussed the multiple areas in which Mario has experienced homophobia: with peers, with potential romantic partners, with his father and in society. These multiple sources led to withdrawal (i.e., school avoidance) and brittle, narcissistic defenses to mask his fear of not being valued as a gay boy. Attention to issues related to feeling welcomed by me, awareness of the effects of rejection for his sexuality, and a particular necessity for openness in relation to discussing sexuality are important aspects of the treatment. For some gay teens, therapy may be the first setting in which a facilitating environment, an atmosphere of openness to the exploration of all aspects of the self, may be experienced. I have also tried to convey the way that my concerns regarding 'normativity' led at times to a cautious exploration of this boy's sexuality.

As adolescents experiment, they need adults around them to contain and imagine their developing sexuality. Retrospectively, I was able to understand that Mario's initial fear of catastrophe (the Berlin Wall coming down) represented his terror that his sexuality could break through in an uncontained manner. His association to the Berlin Wall coming down is a poignant one. When he expressed it, the idea was fraught with a sense of sinister forces. The real Berlin Wall, however, was also a perverse, repressive structure that needed to come down in order to reunite parts of a divided city. I believe Mario's metaphor also unconsciously foreshadowed the hope that such a change inside himself, although terrifying, could help to unite parts of himself alienated through internalized homophobia. If sexuality and love are subject to excessive repression or dissociation, as may be more likely for gay teens in homophobic settings, breakthrough experiences can occur (or be feared to occur), subjecting these teens to alarming experiences of disorientation.[16] I believe that once Mario felt that he had a genuine opportunity with me to explore and name his sexuality, his fear of breakdown subsided.[17] Concomitantly, I think Mario was able to gradually construct a more flexible and protective barrier – e.g., he could increasingly discriminate between what was constructive or destructive to take inside himself.

The experience of prejudice presents the person who suffers it a confusion to sort out. Munoz comments:

> I always marvel at the way nonwhite children survive a white supremacist U.S. culture that preys on them. I am equally in awe of the ways queer children navigate a homophobic public sphere that would rather they did not exist.
>
> (1999: 37)

It is hurtful to be hated or rejected, and the experience of hatred or rejection can be conflated with internal struggles, such as Mario's struggle to come to terms with his sexuality. In that sense, internalized homophobia is a particular problem. On the other hand, what adolescent does not have concerns about her or his sexuality? In that sense, Mario's anxiety about 'flesh' is a universal one in adolescence. I sit with any number of adolescents who all of a sudden clamp down because some aspect of their sexuality comes to the fore. Eventually, we may be able to understand what this has to do with beginning to menstruate or having a wet dream or a disturbing fantasy. Mario's horror of flesh might be thought of as representing greater accessibility to the psychotic elements of the personality in adolescence, but there is also an element of the normal in it.

Extreme feelings about one's body are ubiquitous in adolescence. Indicators of health in adolescence would have little to do with extreme feelings or images, but more to do with the gradual and emerging ability to integrate these feelings inside oneself. In that sense, a fear of one's homosexuality is little different than any other adolescent fear of one's flesh. Of course, in any fear or hatred related to the flesh in adolescence there can be more benign or far darker versions. An example of this range would be mild or transient eating problems compared with the destructiveness of serious eating disorders. The acceptance of bodily developments and related fantasies are challenging for all adolescents and are facilitated by their acceptance in analysis, in the family and in society.

The age of coming out is a subject that deserves exploration. Coming out early with the aid of psychotherapy allowed Mario to free himself from social withdrawal and academic decline. Resumption of peer relationships allowed him the experimentation that is crucial in mid-adolescence. On the other hand, coming out earlier than many of his peers left Mario out of step and therefore subject to rejection in romantic relationships with boys who were not yet ready to come out themselves. Coming out is an intensely individual matter. Our role as analysts is to help our patients freely explore their sexuality. I believe that although coming out at a young age posed some difficulties for Mario, overall, it allowed him to take up the task of discovering his authentic self. Coming out at a later age can leave young adults with a feeling of having "missed out" on key adolescent experiences (Brady & Tyminski, 2009). As I discussed in the Introduction to this book, adolescence is a phase when 'things happen' and they happen in real time,' e.g., the first wet dream, first menstruation or the first boyfriend or girlfriend. Mario's choice to name his sexuality allowed him to engage in adolescence in a manner that added to his vitality and allowed him the opportunity for the bumps, bruises and glories of adolescence that we all deserve.

## Acknowledgment

An earlier version of this chapter was presented on January 14, 2010, at the American Psychoanalytic Association Meetings, New York. The paper won the 2010 Ralph E. Roughton Award of the American Psychoanalytic Association for Outstanding Contribution to the Psychoanalytic Literature on Homosexuality. First published as: Brady, M.T. (2011). "Sometimes we are prejudiced against ourselves": Internalized and external homophobia in the treatment of an adolescent boy. *Contemporary Psychoanalysis, 47*(4): 458–479. Reprinted by permission of Taylor & Francis, LLC.

## Notes

1 There has been important work on normative homosexual identity formation done by non-psychoanalysts. See, e.g., Cass (1979), Troiden (1988), Martin (1991), and Savin-Williams (2005).

2 Increasing depictions of gay lives in the media are of some help to gay teens in conceptualizing their futures. Denizet-Lewis (2009) described the positive influence of the Internet on gay middle schoolers: "Going online broke through the isolation that had been hallmark of being young and gay" (39). Also of note are the "It gets better" video archives accessible to gay teens on YouTube. Gay adolescents, however, are still at a disadvantage when they do not have the opportunity to make the fumbling, awkward approaches to trying on aspects of identity and eroticism like their heterosexual peers.

3 *Psychotic* is employed here in Laufer's usage (1986) of psychotic manifestations in adolescence as distinguished from adult psychoses. Psychotic behavior and thought in adolescence must be understood in relation to the psychic strains of integrating new bodily capacities. Laufer considers adolescent psychotic phenomena to be parallel to adult psychoses only when the "adolescent has lost the ability to doubt" (1986: 370).

4 The dynamic meanings of Mario's horror of 'flesh' were not clear at this point, although the intensity of his revulsion raised questions regarding psychotic aspects of his personality. One of the challenges – and interests – in treating adolescents is that their personalities are far more fluid than those of adults, and issues must be viewed with uncertainty regarding their transience or potential for more ongoing pathological significance. All teenagers are struggling with rapid bodily changes and these conflicts can spill over into the bodily-based symptoms characteristic of adolescence, e.g., eating disorders, substance abuse and cutting (Brady, 2016).

5 Denizet-Lewis reports (2009: 39) that at least 120 middle schools across the country have formed 'Gay Straight Alliance Groups' (GSAs) where gay and lesbian students and their straight peers meet to address anti-gay bullying and harassment. It is worth noting that Mario participated in the GSA at his middle

school. The increase of GSAs in middle schools and high schools shows that these schools envision that some of their students are gay. The existence of these organizations makes it less burdensome to come out and may contribute to an eventual decrease in suicide rates amongst gay teens.

6 Proposition 8 was a California ballot proposition and a state constitutional amendment passed in the November 2008 California elections. The proposition was created by opponents of same-sex marriage. Proposition 8 was ultimately ruled unconstitutional by a federal court in 2010, although the court decision did not go into effect until mid-2013, following the conclusion of appeals. In 2015 the U.S. Supreme Court held in the landmark *Obergefell v. Hodges* that the fundamental right to marry is guaranteed to same-sex couples.

7 Mario will also need to work to keep himself safe, including – but not exclusively – in regard to his sexuality (e.g., practicing safe sex and reading his environment to determine how safe it is to be openly gay). One current developmental issue is whether the facilitating environment (including me) can convey a sense that he is worthy of protection. This sense of value and protection can gradually be internalized into adequate self-protection.

8 I encountered a similar problem when teaching psychoanalytic developmental theory. Some conceptualization of what is 'normal' is implicit in all developmental theories. These issues have been famously fraught in relation to female development and increasingly so in relation to homosexual development. It is incumbent upon analytic institutes to teach developmental theory within frameworks that question the normativities involved, or else we are in danger of proliferating misogynistic and homophobic developmental theories.

9 This citation is an example of Blechner's observation that although homophobia in psychoanalytic writing is less stark than it used to be, it can be "even more problematic . . . [when] well-meaning psychoanalysts often do not recognize their biases and the way their conceptions of mental health conformed to the prejudices of society at large" (1993a: 630). I recognize that the developmental references I cite could be viewed as dated. All of these citations, however, were part of the required reading in my training in child analysis. Part of what is best about psychoanalysis is that wisdom is passed down from generation to generation. Prized theories of the previous generations are transmitted to candidates. Our internalization of theories is partly an identification with teachers and necessarily partly emotional. However, this handing down from generation to generation is relevant to why issues such as homophobia in psychoanalytic theory are slow to change and cannot be claimed to have changed fully because there may be less obvious examples in current literature.

10 Drescher describes Freud's "theory of immaturity" as one that "juvenilizes diverse sexualities" (2007: 219).

11 Freud never fully resolved the tension in his thinking between biological essentialism (i.e., anatomy is destiny) and a radical view of the centrality of psychic bisexuality. There has been a subsequent argument in the literature on

psychic bisexuality regarding its role as primary or defensive (against a sense of loss of omnipotence). My own view echoes Winnicott's sense of bisexuality as an area of play or transitional space, which is potentially neither concrete nor delusional. Like Corbett's "girlyboys", Mario seemed to value his penis and maleness while playing with identifications culturally associated with femininity.

12 Other meanings of his more masculine dress could also be considered, such as an adaptation to his high school environment or to the wishes of his current boyfriend, or even to rejecting important aspects of himself.

13 'Adolescent and analyst at work in the present space' panel, International Psychoanalytic Association 46th Congress, July 30, 2009, Chicago, IL.

14 Denizet-Lewis quotes Eileen Ross, the director of the Outlet program, a support service for gay youth in Mountain View, California, saying: "No one says to [heterosexual boys]: 'Are you sure? You're too young to know if you like girls. It's probably just a phase.' But that's what we say too often to gay youth. We deny them their feelings and truth in a way we would never do with a heterosexual young person" (Denizet-Lewis, 2009: 39). On this point, see also Cass (1979), Martin (1991) and Troiden (1988).

15 For an exception to this silence, albeit not in the journals Moss cites, see Blechner (1993b, 1997).

16 I am aware that Mario's early, and seemingly certain, consolidation of his sexual identity could be viewed as a defense against underlying confusion, disorganization and psychotic thinking. There may be some element of truth to this view. His early naming of his sexuality, however, did not lead to a sense that threatening parts of himself had been further dissociated – and were therefore more dangerous. Instead, there was a sense that the danger had been reduced because a seemingly dangerous part of his self (i.e., the sexuality he feared was unacceptable to himself and others) was allowed to come forward.

17 I do not mean to imply that Mario's dread regarding his homosexuality was the only reason for his fear of a breakdown. But, the strains of adolescence that make this period especially vulnerable to breakdown are increased when teens' efforts to wall off their sexuality are heightened by internal or external homophobia.

## References

American Psychoanalytic Association. (1999). Minutes of the meeting of the Executive Council, December 16. New York: American Psychoanalytic Association.

Barredo, C. (2009). Discussion of Mary Brady's clinical material, during 'Adolescent and analyst at work in the present space' panel at the International Psychoanalytic Association 46th Congress, July 30, Chicago, IL.

Blechner, M.J. (1993a). Homophobia in psychoanalytic writing and practice: Commentary on Trop and Stolorow's 'Defense analysis in self psychology:

A developmental view' and Hanna's 'False-self sensitivity to countertransference: Anatomy of a single session.' *Psychoanalytic Dialogues, 3*: 627–637.

Blechner, M.J. (1993b). Psychoanalysis and HIV disease. *Contemporary Psychoanalysis, 29*: 61–80.

Blechner, M.J. (1997). *Hope and Mortality: Psychodynamic Approaches to AIDS and HIV*. Hillsdale, NJ: Analytic Press.

Blos, P. (1962). *On Adolescence*. New York: Free Press.

Brady, M.T. (2016). *The Body in Adolescence: Psychic Isolation and Physical Symptoms*. London: Routledge.

Brady, M., & Tyminski, R. (2009). Internalized homophobia. *Paper given at the National Meeting of the American College Health Association*, May 28, San Francisco, CA.

Cass, V. (1979). Homosexual identity formation: A theoretical model. *Journal of Homosexuality, 4*(3): 219–235.

Corbett, K. (1996). Homosexual boyhood: Notes on girlyboys. *Gender & Psychoanalysis, 2*: 429–461.

Corbett, K. (2001). More life: Centrality and marginality in human development. *Psychoanalytic Dialogues, 11*: 313–335.

Denizet-Lewis, B. (2009). Coming out in middle school. *Sunday New York Times Magazine*, September 27: 36–55.

Drescher, J. (2007). From bisexuality to intersexuality: Rethinking gender categories. *Contemporary Psychoanalysis, 43*: 204–228.

Fonagy, P., Gergely, G., Jurist, E., & Target, M. (2002). *Affect Regulation, Mentalization and the Development of Self*. New York: Other Press.

Freud, S. (1905). Three essays on the theory of sexuality. *Standard Edition*, Vol. 7: 125–148. London: Hogarth Press.

Friedman, R., & Downey, J. (2002). *Sexual Orientations and Psychoanalysis: Sexual Science and Clinical Practice*. New York, NY: Columbia University Press.

Harley, M. (1970). On some problems of technique in the analysis of early adolescents. *Psychoanalytic Study of the Child, 25*: 99–121.

Harris, A. (1996). Animated conversation: Embodying and gendering. *Gender & Psychoanalysis, 1*: 361–383.

Hegna, K. (2007). Coming out, coming into what? Identification and risks in the 'coming out' story of a Norwegian late adolescent gay man. *Sexualities, 10*(5): 582–602.

Isay, R. (1989). Adolescence and young adulthood of gay men. In *Being Homosexual: Gay Men and their Development*. New York: Farrar Straus Giroux, pp. 47–66.

Klein, M. (1922). Inhibitions and difficulties at puberty. In *Love, Guilt & Reparation and Other Works*. New York: Free Press, pp. 54–59.

Laufer, M. (1986). Adolescence and psychosis. *International Journal of Psychoanalysis, 67*: 367–372.

Levy-Warren, M. (1996). Middle adolescent genitality: Gender and sexuality in the world of peers. In *The Adolescent Journey*. New York: Jason Aronson, pp. 69–100.

Lingiardi, V. (2001). Ars erotica or scientia sexualis? Post-Jungian reflections on the homosexualities. *Journal of Gay & Lesbian Psychotherapy, 5*: 29–57.

Malyon, A. (1982). Psychotherapeutic implications of internalized homophobia in gay men. *Journal of Homosexuality, 7*: 59–69.

Martin, H. (1991). The coming-out process for homosexuals. *Hospital & Community Psychiatry, 42*: 158–162.

Moss, D. (1997). On situating homophobia. *Journal of the American Psychoanalytic Association, 45*: 201–215.

Moss, D. (2002). Internalized homophobia in men: Wanting in the first person singular, hating in the first-person plural. *Psychoanalytic Quarterly, 71*: 21–50.

Munoz, J.D. (1999). *Disidentifications: Queers of color and the performance of politics*. Minneapolis, MN: University of Minnesota Press.

Phillips, S. (2001). The overstimulation of everyday life: I. New aspects of male homosexuality. *Journal of the American Psychoanalytic Association, 49*: 1235–1267.

Phillips, S. (2002). The overstimulation of everyday life: II. Male homosexuality, countertransference, and psychoanalytic treatment. *Annual Psychoanalysis, 30*: 131–145.

Reis, B. (2003). Relational perspectives in psychoanalysis. *Journal of the American Psychoanalytic Association, 51*: 295–300.

Roughton, R. (2002). Rethinking homosexuality: What it teaches us about psychoanalysis. *Journal of the American Psychoanalytic Association, 50*: 733–763.

Savin-Williams, R. (2005). *The New Gay Teenager*. Cambridge, MA: Harvard University Press.

Straker, G. (2006). The anti-analytic third. *Psychoanalytic Review, 93*: 729–753.

Troiden, R. (1988). Homosexual identity development. *Journal of Adolescent Health Care, 9*: 105–113.

Tyson, P., & Tyson, R. (1990). *Psychoanalytic Theories of Development*. New Haven, CT: Yale University Press.

Winnicott, D. (1961). Contemporary concepts of adolescent development and their implications for higher education. In *Playing and Reality* (1985). London: Tavistock, pp. 138–150.

Winnicott, D. (1965). *The Maturational Processes and the Facilitating Environment*. New York: International Universities Press.

# Chapter 3

# 'Sleeping beauties'

## Succession problems of adolescence

[I]t is the analyst who becomes 'the setting of possible fairy tales and play.' He lends himself to all the emotional roles required by the field, roles which can subsequently be thought about again and verbalized, once they have been transformed in the analyst's working-through.

(Ferro, 1999: 57)

Certain adolescents present to us as 'sleeping beauties,' seemingly free of severe symptomatology or of the acting out characteristic of adolescence. As analysts we can be lulled to sleep by their somnolence. Seemingly not much is wrong, and yet there is an absence of passion, including in the analytic process. This chapter conveys adolescent turbulence in inverse – too hot to handle and thus slept through.

In this chapter I will discuss the fairy tale *Sleeping Beauty* as well as my clinical experience with such 'sleeping beauties.' I will consider the succession process of adolescence, the psychic isolation (Brady, 2016) experienced during that phase and the splitting required to manage the conflicting desires of adolescence. My aim is to discuss normative aspects of adolescence, which can yet become entrenched and preventive of growth. Persistent and pervasive avoidance of the turbulence of adolescence constitutes a psychic retreat (Steiner, 1993) from the adolescent process. I also aim to discuss the conflicting feelings of the older generation (parents and analysts) toward adolescents.

Since the birth of psychoanalysis, analysts have used myths or tales as a way to capture and convey fundamental truths about human nature and relationships. Likewise, fairy tales have been described (Bettelheim, 1975) as providing a unique way for children to come to terms with the dilemmas of their inner worlds.[1]

Developments in analysis over recent years emphasize the nourishment of the analyst's and the patient's creativity. Ferro (1999) describes the use of "narrative derivatives" to assist the growth of the mind, suggesting that a patient's comment on a fairy tale, film, etc., allows imaginative elaboration of unconscious conflicts in the patient and in the analytic field, which can lay the groundwork for more direct interpretation. The shared elaboration between patient and analyst gradually assists both minds to grow to name and handle conflicts. While the interpretation of conflict is important, the growth of the capacity to handle intense emotions and the processes of reverie in the analyst have become more central in much contemporary psychoanalytic thinking (Bion, 1962; Ogden, 1997; Ferro, 1999).

I will first recap the tale of *Sleeping Beauty* and then link it to the succession process of adolescence. This process occurs in the adolescent, but also reciprocally in the analyst and the parents.

## Sleeping Beauty

In the Brothers Grimm's *Sleeping Beauty* (1917), the King and Queen invite seven fairies to come to their daughter's christening. Each of the fairies is given "a plate with a spoon, a knife and a fork – all pure gold. But alas!" – a very old fairy has been forgotten. The King invites her to be seated but is unable to furnish a gold table setting for her. This makes the old fairy angry. She spitefully casts a spell: "When the princess is 17 years old, she shall prick her finger with a spindle and-she-shall-die!"[2]

Fortunately, a young fairy comes to the rescue. She cannot

> undo what my elder sister has done: the princess shall indeed prick her finger with a spindle, but she shall not die. She shall fall into sleep that will last a hundred years. At the end of that time, a king's son will find her and awaken her.
>
> (Grimm & Grimm, 1917)

Despite the King's command that all spindles be burned, one old woman too deaf to hear the command continues to spin with her spindle. At the age of 17, Sleeping Beauty comes upon the old woman and wants to try her hand at spinning. She does indeed prick her finger and goes to sleep for 100 years. The good fairy knows that Sleeping Beauty will be frightened when she awakens if she finds herself alone, so she casts a spell on all the others in the castle, except the King and Queen, to likewise go to sleep. The King and Queen depart the castle and later die. A wood springs up around the castle, impenetrable by man or beast. Later, of course, a brave, young prince learns of the prophecy. He makes his way to the castle and awakens Sleeping Beauty with a kiss. The rest of the castle inhabitants awaken and return to what they were doing. And in the end, Sleeping Beauty and the Prince wed, move to the Prince's father's castle and live happily ever after.

## Succession problems of adolescence

I envision *Sleeping Beauty* as capturing the succession problems of adolescence for both the new and the old generations. In order for the adolescent to attain adulthood, there must be a shift in the generations. As Loewald (1980) tells us, this involves in some sense the murder of the parents. However, I see the psychological murder of the parents as one crucial aspect, but only one aspect of the problem of the passage of generations. In the arduous process of development adolescents want to kill their parents *and* to keep them alive. The adolescent splits off his need to murder the older generation from his love for his parents. In splitting off aggressive parts they are less integrated and feel potentially more dangerous.

The splitting and idealization fundamental to healthy development in the infant are also characteristic of adolescence. The good object/self is idealized in order to stave off anxiety and confusion. This categorical and rigid separation between good and bad can yield to a gradual reintegration of split-off aspects. Meltzer (1973) comments that the values of the paranoid-schizoid position are gradually replaced by the values of the depressive position, and egocentricity yields to concern for loved objects in our internal and external world:

> The gradual shift in values has a sweeping effect upon judgment and the estimation in which are held the various attributes of human nature. Thus goodness, beauty, strength and generosity replace in esteem the initial enthrallment to size, power, success and sensuality.
>
> (224)

I have written elsewhere (Brady, 2016) about the physical symptoms (e.g., eating disorders, cutting and substance abuse) that can emerge in adolescence and express the unnamable physical and emotional tumult of this phase. Here I am considering a different adolescent syndrome: that in which adolescent developmental upheaval is avoided or slept through to a greater or lesser degree. Perhaps all adolescents sleep through that which they cannot deal with to some extent. I think of a late adolescent boy who treated me like a comfortable couch; I would be there when he needed me, and he didn't need to think of me otherwise. If he missed a session he did not wonder what I might feel about it. I did not seem to have emerged in his mind as a person in my own right even two years into twice-weekly therapy. I pointed out that I seemed like 'background' to him. He noticed that he treated his own parents in a similar manner. He acknowledged that he had 'won the parent lottery' when he compared his patient, responsible parents with his girlfriend's rather immature mother and father.

We could imagine a range of narcissistic or aggressive reasons for a young person's inability to imagine an analyst as a separate person. But I am thinking of this late adolescent as sleeping through or forestalling the separation process. If I emerge as a separate person for him, then he is also more of a separate person instead of asleep to any question of separation or loss.

Some adolescents may present with combinations of psychic somnolence and physical symptoms. Could we think of anorexia, for instance, as, in part, a girl's unconscious effort to weaken herself, in order to sleep through the desire to succeed mother? Weakening oneself/sleeping could prevent the physical growth into womanhood that can unconsciously be experienced as killing mother. Such a deadly symptom is surely a fraught combination of violence and protection (Rey, 1994).

Meltzer discusses the "apprehension" (in both meanings of the word) of beauty in an anorexic patient. Consciously the patient sees the beauty of her object/mother and the beauty in the world. But "in the persecutory component of the experience she feels the beauty to be merely a screen for the greedy and cruel fingers of the witch-mother reaching into her to snatch away her vitality and scratch away her beauty" (1973: 226). From this point of view sleep could be a girl's way to withdraw from the witch-mother's hatred of her developing beauty and to preserve the beauty of self/mother in a timeless sleep.

In the poet Anne Sexton's mordant retelling of 'Briar Rose (Sleeping Beauty)', the forgotten old fairy is described much as the above patient's 'witch-mother':

her fingers as long and thin as straws
her eyes burnt by cigarettes,
her uterus an empty teacup

(Sexton, 1971/1988: 169)

But, in Sexton's literary rendering, sleep is also submission/escape from a dangerous father:

I was passed hand to hand
Like a bowl of fruit.
Each night I am nailed into place and forget who I am.
Daddy?

(Sexton, 1971/1988: 173)

I consider the experience of "psychic isolation" (Brady, 2016) to be characteristic of adolescence, as teenagers are often not yet ready to integrate or articulate newfound physiologic capacities and concomitant emotions and fantasies. Erikson's (1959) concept of adolescent "moratorium" as well as Winnicott's (1965) adolescent "doldrums" come to mind. The psychological work of adolescence is too great to be gone through in any efficient manner. The adolescent often feels cut off from his or her younger self and not yet able to see a way toward an older self.

The adolescent process cannot be sped up, so the imagery of sleeping for 100 years is apt. Bettelheim comments:

While many fairy tales stress great deeds the heroes must perform to become themselves, 'The Sleeping Beauty' emphasizes the long, quiet concentration on oneself that is also needed. During the months before the first menstruation, and often also for some time immediately following it, girls are passive, seem sleepy, and withdraw into themselves. While no equally noticeable state heralds the coming of sexual maturity in boys, many of them experience a period of lassitude and of turning inward during puberty which equals the female experience.

(1975: 225)

This sleep is ultimately pierced by the development toward sexual love, but this transition involves the pain of loss of childhood. A 14-year-old boy starting his first sexual relationship told me he was afraid he would no longer love Christmas with his parents in the same way he always had.

It is familiar and convincing to consider the prick of the needle as representing the dawning awareness of sexual penetration and menstrual/reproductive functioning. This view is persuasive, but the prick with the needle also seems an unconscious association to the first prick of awareness of the desire to supplant the older generation (making the old woman irrelevant by taking over the spinning, or making parents less central by becoming sexually mature oneself).[3] While the imagery of being penetrated and bleeding is more directly relevant to female development, males are also pierced by love and loss.

Sleep, of course, is a state in which dreams occur. We could imagine Sleeping Beauty dreaming her own tale of love and loss. All of these developments take time, so the 100 years are needed before a full awakening can occur. By the end of the story Sleeping Beauty's parents are dead, she awakens to sexual love and she moves to the Prince's father's palace. It was interesting to note that the Brothers Grimm have the couple move to the Prince's father's palace instead of to their own castle. Perhaps this represents the late adolescent's developmental need that parents remain, while there is a fundamental change of function. Parents are killed and yet survive.

## Succession problems for parents of adolescents

*Sleeping Beauty* begins: "Once upon a time there lived a king and queen who were very unhappy because they had no children. But at last a little daughter was born, and their sorrow was turned to joy" (Grimm and Grimm, 1917). The adult world (the King and Queen) long for a new generation. We both provide for it (the good fairies) and resent and envy it (the old fairy). Bettelheim sees *Sleeping Beauty* as representing parents' inevitable failure to prevent their child's sexual awakening (1975: 30). Adolescents frequently make parents feel old and irrelevant as they experience themselves as discovering sexuality for the first time.

The old fairy represents the parental generation's hatred of the young for supplanting us and claiming what was once ours – budding sexuality, early promise, physical youth, etc. If parents are not willing to be sidelined to some degree, we cannot take up the promise of parenthood – to be transformed by our love for our children. The young fairy could be the aspect of the older generation that sympathizes with the challenges of youth and is able to feel renewed by the cyclical process of life. The King and Queen (in part) inhabit the depressive position. The King and Queen leave the castle after Sleeping Beauty is put to sleep. Parents must leave the territory and position we have previously occupied and go in search of other ways to be ourselves. Despite their seeming power and effort they are not able to protect their daughter from the spell, not able to prevent the progression of generations or their own deaths. On the other hand, the King's rejection of the old fairy (forgetting her 'place') also reflects our potential to split off and deny ageing and envy. The older generation's inability to integrate ageing and loss could leave adolescents more fearful to face the succession of generations.

The sleeping servants surrounding Sleeping Beauty evoke the cut-off quality possible between adults and children in the face of adolescents' developing bodies. I have been struck when meeting with some parents of adolescents by how little they know about their children. This is due, in part, to the adolescent's developmentally normative withdrawal from the parents. But not only so – the adolescent's sexual development and sub-jective emotional states can be more than a parent wants or can bear to have contact with. Likewise, parents can experience their adolescent's changes as a portent of the loss of their youth. The parents of an adoles-cent boy come to mind. The mother seemed to have gone into a depressive sleep and relegated emotional contact with her son to me. The father, on the other hand, seemed stimulated by his son's adolescence and to be in a fully-fledged adolescent state himself.

## Aside

My interest in *Sleeping Beauty* was aroused while preparing a discussion of a paper by Ungar (2014) entitled 'What remains and what has changed in psychoanalysis.'[4] Ungar suggests that our theory changes in relation to changes in the culture, and that adolescents are the group most affected by rapid cultural changes. She also suggests that adolescents are more alone than ever before. I have discussed an affective sense of psychic isolation as an essential element of adolescence (Brady, 2016). It would seem that all adolescents suffer the strangeness of bodily changes somewhat alone. And yet some elements of adolescent loneliness are contemporary devel-opments. Pressures on contemporary adolescents can leave them very lit-tle room for an inner, intimate space. Many adolescents I work with are highly scheduled and are in settings over-focused on external markers of success. Their need for a seemingly timeless sleep, which allows them to absorb their changes, is largely neglected.

The absence of intimate spaces abandons adolescents into more narcissistic formations. Much has been written (e.g., Mondzrak, 2012) suggesting a contemporary culture of narcissism. Part of this culture of narcissism is the idealization of youth. Consequently, parents may find it harder to parent if they need to deny the loss of their own youth and the transition of generations. Generational differences and conflicts crucial to adolescent identity building may be avoided (slept through).

Ungar provides a clinical vignette of a 15-year-old girl she calls 'Griselda' who says:

> "I don't get on well with guys – I don't have a single male friend. I don't like the places we go out to at night and I don't drink alcohol – it makes me feel bad right away and the smell of vomit in those places revolts me. I don't dare try a joint . . ."
>
> (2014)

Ungar recommends that Griselda start analysis

> based on the idea that she needed to be accompanied during this adolescent process . . . And on the fact that she seemed to me to be too involved in the world of adults, without, as she herself said, "finding [her] place."
>
> (2014)

Ungar reports a session in the third year of analysis, in which Griselda (now 18) complains that her friends are not interested in her life but just stop at her house because it is convenient for night clubs. Ungar interprets that Griselda feels it is difficult for her analyst to understand how bad she felt when faced with such changes. Griselda's "reaction was quite violent, saying that for sure I didn't understand, that I had already passed through these moments but, as it was such a long time ago, I didn't remember how it felt" (2014: 12–13). Griselda ended this session however, noticing that her boyfriend has started to matter to her.

In the next session Griselda tells Ungar that her boyfriend has received a negative HIV test result and asks: "[C]an I stop using rubbers now?" Ungar replies that "it's not just about whether you use a rubber or not" but "that you started your sex life . . . A lot of issues come up: how you feel, the necessity of intimacy, for example" (2014: 13). In an irritated manner, Griselda complains she has nothing more to say: "[T]his free association thing seems just dumb. For example . . . we can hear the birds singing. So what?" Ungar perseveres and says: "[F]or example, you could try to think about what comes to mind when you hear the birdsong." Griselda replies:

> "Okay, I've thought of some stupidity: I remembered the film *Sleeping Beauty*. She was dancing in a garden in a pink princess dress and, in the film – I don't know if you saw it – there were two little birds singing, the two of them sitting on a branch, one was pink and the other was light blue."
>
> (2014)

Ungar interprets to Griselda that "The time in which Sleeping Beauty is asleep" is similar to Griselda's life – "a time of suffering when you realize that you are lost in the world of adults and of obligations and responsibilities." Griselda confirms Dr. Ungar's interpretation, responding:

> "How nice it would be to go to sleep and wake up having passed all the bad part. I'm not in any rush to get older, but I never imagined that something that I was really wanting to happen – like finish high school, find a boyfriend, start university – was going to cause such a mess in my life."
>
> (2014)

I will now discuss my patient, 'Laura,' who I experienced as in a protracted avoidance of adolescent turbulence.

## Laura

Laura, aged 15, came to treatment at the recommendation of her high school counsellor, who saw her as highly needy of adults at school and out of step with her peers. Laura's parents had divorced two years earlier. When I first spoke on the phone with Laura's parents I discussed with them whether Laura might want to come in first to meet with me to tell her story. Laura's parents felt that she would want to do so. When I met with Laura she was adamant that I should not meet with her parents.

She seemed cynical about either my or her parents' ability to handle such a meeting in a respectful or protective manner. I acknowledged her concerns but ultimately told her I would need to meet with her parents at least once or twice to ensure that we had a working agreement that would allow the treatment to proceed.

Laura's parents did not want to meet jointly, so I met with them separately. Deep divisions, resentments and a potential to fight over the treatment were evident. Father seemed highly skeptical of treatment for Laura as he felt mother's therapy had not helped her at all and had contributed to the divorce. I thought that he was concerned I would turn his daughter against him. I emphasized the need for the treatment to be a conflict-free zone so that Laura could really use it. I was dubious about this arrangement holding, but Laura remained adamant that she did not want her parents' involvement. Thankfully, the parents did not fight over the twice-weekly treatment and continued to support it over the following years. Also, thankfully, the intensity of acrimony between the parents seemed to subside over time and they seemed (to differing degrees) to be able to get on with their own lives.

Laura agreed to twice-weekly therapy grudgingly. I felt that I would need to be the one to hold the value of treatment in mind for her and that she would not risk emotional vulnerability. Early in treatment Laura acknowledged some self-destructive ideas such as having a strong feeling of wanting to swerve her car off the road and crash. Mainly, however, she seemed quite identified with the adults at her high school and to be avoiding an adolescent process. She was frequently in roles where she had authority over other adolescents who seemed to find her uptight and controlling. She told me: "I feel like I like people more than they like me." My experience was that she wanted to feel chosen by me without putting herself on the line.

Despite her minimization of the treatment, Laura remained in therapy throughout the rest of high school and wanted to continue on the phone on a once-a-week basis when she began college. We continued to meet in person when she returned home for vacations.

While we had both gone to some effort to continue to meet together, Laura continued to diminish the importance of our work. She frequently talked about practical matters, choices of classes, internships, etc. I felt somewhat bored and restricted from a more dimensional, evocative or intimate involvement.

I felt I could begin to challenge Laura's minimization of me, as significant work had been done about her distrust of adults however my emotional experience was of continuing to be turned down in my invitation to more intimate involvement.[5] Meanwhile, Laura had only minimally entered into romantic relationships with men and not at all with women. Her sexual orientation did not seem evident. "I am not going there," was her response when issues emerged in her friendships. She was a reasonable student, but often found herself bored by her course work.

I raised the idea of returning to our twice-weekly meetings, but Laura was unwilling. In fact, she wanted to take a break from the treatment as she had a summer internship in another state. I interpreted that she was avoiding a more direct emotional involvement with me, but did agree to the break. In our first phone session after the break, Laura cried when she heard my voice. She said that I listened to her in a way that was different from anyone else. Although she was quick to dismiss the importance of her feeling, I thought that she had had a developmental experience of doing without me, but finding that she missed me. I told Laura that while I had been willing to carry the value of our work for some time, I thought her unwillingness to see my importance to her was no longer useful to her. I said that while she frequently viewed my wish to meet more often as an effort to control her, my experience was that she often turned me down. I said I thought that this must also be how other people found her – unwilling to really enter in a relationship. I had been the King and Queen who must let her sleep, but now I felt like the Prince who must insist on her coming to life.[6]

My insistence on intimacy with Laura was followed by her gradually increasing her ability to maintain relationships with friends during conflicts, and then to her first romantic and sexual relationship with a young man. As she spoke of these wonderful and awkward moments, my memories of these times in my own life were stimulated. Although I felt that I needed to pierce my patient's sleep (the analyst as the Prince), I also found that when Laura had found her own Prince in the external world, I had to be willing to acknowledge this development. I needed to be willing to cede the centrality of my role with Laura, but not so quickly as to leave her waking up by herself.

## Discussion

Use of the characters in a fairy tale allows an analyst to play with the different roles the patient unconsciously assigns her. I felt for a time like the

King and Queen who must bear the 100-year sleep of a patient who denied her own desires. Eventually I felt that I must break through this denial, penetrating the wood surrounding her, yet at a time I hoped, when she was psychologically ready for me to do so.

I am not trying to suggest that a clinical situation will unfold like the text of any fairy tale, including *Sleeping Beauty*. I agree with Ferro that "the characteristic of the psychoanalytic situation is that it confronts two living texts which interreact and transform each other" (1999: 115). Listening to an hour like a fairy tale or a dream, though, can sustain the analyst's ability to imaginatively engage with the shifting subjectivities in our patient and in our self.

Campanile distinguishes between subjectivation in adolescence – the ability to recognize and represent what one feels – from subjectivization, which he calls the process of recognition by the subject of "the multiplicity and relativity of the subjects that each individual has within himself." He comments on the double sense of the term 'subject,' particularly in adolescence, the sense of "an author and of one who is subjugated, subjected to forces and mechanisms that he can learn to see and recognize" (2012: 416). My patient and I evolved from her need to be desired without having to risk desire herself, to braving ownership of her own desires. Such subjective experiences are not static but constantly evolving, as were my own subjective experiences of being with Laura. The elasticity of the fairy tale allows either the analyst in her reverie, or the patient and analyst together, to imagine a changing subjective narrative.

Feminist critiques of *Sleeping Beauty* see the tale as imparting patriarchal social norms (e.g., Semsar, 2014). In contrast, Bettelheim (1975) sees the inward turning depicted by Sleeping Beauty and the heroic quest of the Prince as together symbolizing the development of a mature self. He proposes that the ability to negotiate an internal reflective space and to prove oneself in the external world are both necessary elements of adolescence. While *Sleeping Beauty* can be interpreted in this psychically bisexual manner, the cultural critique of roles allowed/imagined for girls is crucial. When choices are restricted, girls might have little chance to imagine themselves into an active, heroic character.

Likewise, what happens when there is "a lack in cultural reverie, a sense of void" (Gonzales, 2013: 117) in gay teenagers' experience of receptivity in their family or culture? Here, the 'animating kiss' of the analyst may be needed to help imagine and enliven the developing gay adolescent's sexuality. The potential avoidance of the emotional turbulence of the adolescent process is relevant for both boys and girls, gay and straight. A genuine awakening in adolescence would involve not just joining stereotypic and proscribed cultural roles, but grappling with these roles to make them one's own or remaking them when they are oppressive.

## Concluding comments

The succession of generations poses many challenges for the adolescent. I have used *Sleeping Beauty* to capture the normative adolescent "doldrums" (Winnicott, 1965), "moratorium" (Erikson, 1959) or sense of "psychic isolation" (Brady, 2015, 2016). The extreme avoidance of adolescent turbulence constitutes a psychic retreat. The analyst may eventually need to wake an adolescent from such a sleep.

I have commented on the splitting that can characterize the younger and the older generations' reactions to the passage of generations. *Sleeping Beauty* affords us an opportunity to ponder many splits: desire to kill the older generation and keep us alive; envy/hatred of the younger generation and grateful appreciation of the regeneration they can afford us; sexual awakening and death; fearful apprehension of beauty and deeply appreciative apprehension of beauty; joy and grief.

The deep meanings of *Sleeping Beauty* may be best captured by Meltzer's thoughts on the "apprehension of beauty" (1973: 225). Meltzer observes a "failure of apprehension of beauty" in some patients, who lack a "direct and immediate emotional response," and thus are "deprived both of confidence in their judgement as well as in the sincerity of their interest" (1973: 225). He describes the touching termination of a patient who had lost his father when young:

> He was struggling to hold together within himself the joy and pain of the truth about living and not living things, of the frailty and the feebleness of life forces pitted against the malignant, which so often seemed to be favoured by the great random factor. In other words he was seeming to shift his perception of beauty from the idealized good object to the struggle itself, thus including the malign and the random, along with the good, as participants in the drama, and thus in his love of the world.
>
> (1973: 226)

Thus, *Sleeping Beauty* offers us a reflection on the possibility of 'apprehending' (both fearing and appreciating) the beauties of the passage of generations and the passage of time, which are central to human existence.

## Acknowledgments

First published as: Brady, M.T. (2017): 'Sleeping beauties': succession problems of adolescence. *Journal of Child Psychotherapy, 43*(1): 55–65. Reprinted by permission of Taylor & Francis, LLC.

Excerpts from 'Briar Rose (Sleeping Beauty)' from TRANSFORMATIONS by Anne Sexton. Copyright © 1971 by Anne Sexton. Reprinted by permission of Houghton Mifflin Company. All Rights Reserved.

## Notes

1 See Bettelheim (1975) for the antecedent versions of the Brothers Grimm version of *Sleeping Beauty*. See also Ben-Amos (1994) for a folklorist's critique of psychoanalytic interpretations of fairy tales. I am not claiming any insight into the author's intentions, nor of the way the tale may have been interpreted when it was written. I am simply advocating the mobile use of the possible meanings of various characters in fairy tales as they lend themselves to the analyst's reverie.
2 Bettelheim makes a case for the 'curse' as referring to menstruation (1975: 232). From this point of view, Sleeping Beauty is overcome by the experience of sudden bleeding and falls into a long sleep. She is protected from premature intercourse by the wall of thorns.
3 While I see the challenge of burgeoning sexuality as crucial to the meanings of *Sleeping Beauty*, psychosexual development is intimately tied to separation issues for both adolescents and their parents. The emergence of adolescent sexuality portends the emergence of the new generation and the older generation going on toward death.
4 Presented November 15, 2014, at the San Francisco Center for Psychoanalysis, San Francisco, CA.
5 There are movements toward and away from intimacy and its accompanying upheavals with many teenagers, but I experienced Laura as consistently and persistently avoidant of both angry and loving emotions. I would agree with Alvarez, that even with children (or young adults), "chronicity itself has to be addressed" (1992: 57).
6 Alvarez notes that the "normal mother permits and respects some degree of withdrawal on her baby's part, but she also plays, however gently an active part in drawing him back into interaction with her" (1992: 61). I knew that Laura had become disillusioned about intimacy when her family divided, but thought that Laura could become active in reaching toward intimacy in her life.

# References

Alvarez, A. (1992). *Live Company: Psychoanalytic Psychotherapy with Autistic, Borderline, Deprived and Abused Children*. London and New York: Routledge.

Ben-Amos, D. (1994). Bettelheim among the folklorists. *Psychoanalytic Review*, *81*(3): 509–535.

Bettelheim, B. (1975). *The Uses of Enchantment: The Meaning and Importance of Fairy Tales*. New York: Random House.

Bion, W.R. (1962). *Learning from Experience*. London: Karnac.

Brady, M.T. (2015). *The Body in Adolescence: Psychic Isolation and Physical Symptoms*. London and New York: Routledge.

Campanile, P. (2012). "I had twenty-five piercings and pink hair when …": Adolescence, transitional hysteria, and the process of subjectivization. *Psychoanalytic Quarterly*, *81*(2): 401–418. 10.1002/(ISSN)2167-4086

Erikson, E. (1959). *Identity and the Life Cycle. Psychological Issues Monograph 1*. New York: International Universities Press.

Ferro, A. (1999). *The Bi-Personal Field: Experiences in Child Analysis*. London: Routledge.

Gonzales, F. (2013). Another Eden: Proto-gay desire and social precocity. *Studies in Gender and Sexuality*, *14*: 112–121.

Grimm Brothers. (1917). "Sleeping Beauty". Fairy Tales and Other Traditional Stories (Lit2Go Edition). Retrieved October 11, 2014, from http://etc.usf.edu/lit2go/68/fairy-tales-and-other-traditional-stories/5102/sleeping-beauty/

Loewald, H. (1980). The waning of the Oedipus complex. In *Papers on Psychoanalysis*. New Haven, CT: Yale University Press, pp. 384–404.

Meltzer, D. (1973). On the apprehension of beauty. *Contemporary Psychoanalysis*, *9*: 224–229.

Mondzrak, V. (2012). Reflections on psychoanalytic technique with adolescents today: Pseudo-pseudomaturity. *International Journal of Psychoanalysis*, *93*(3): 649–666.

Ogden, T. (1997). Reverie and metaphor: Some thoughts on how I work as a psychoanalyst. *International Journal of Psychoanalysis*, *78*: 719–731.

Rey, H. (1994). Anorexia nervosa. In J. Magagna (Ed.), *Universals of Psychoanalysis in the Treatment of Psychotic and Borderline States*. London: Free Association Books, p. 47–75.

Semsar, S. (2014). Sleeping Beauty through the ages. *Ellipsis*, *41*(31). http://scholarworks.uno.edu/ellipsis/vol41/iss1/31

Sexton, A. (1971/1988). Briar rose (Sleeping Beauty): 169–173. From Transformations: 147–173. In D. Middlebrook & D. George (Eds.), *Selected Poems of Anne Sexton*. Boston, MA: Houghton Mifflin.

Steiner, J. (1993). *Psychic Retreats: Pathological Organizations in Psychotic, Neurotic and Borderline Patients*. London and New York: Routledge.

Ungar, V. (2014). What remains and what has changed in psychoanalysis. *Unpublished paper presented at the Day with Virginia Ungar*, November 15, 2014, San Francisco Center for Psychoanalysis, San Francisco, CA.

Winnicott, D.W. (1965). *The Maturational Processes and the Facilitating Environment: Studies in the Theory of Emotional Development*. London: Hogarth Press/Institute of Psycho-Analysis.

# Chapter 4

# Afflictions related to 'ideals' of masculinity

## Gremlins within

> How would we theorize a masculinity whose cardinal feature is that it be the object of idealization?
>
> (Moss, 2012: 6)

In this chapter I would like to reflect on the nature of a masculine 'ideal,' and how the impossibility of this ideal can foster rigid psychic states. I will argue that the unattainable nature of a masculine ideal can predispose boys and men to inflexible psychic states that can give way to seemingly capricious symptoms and crises of confidence. I am referring to these symptoms as gremlin-like in order to capture their subjective experience as capricious and trouble-making, for instance the seemingly mysterious loss of an erection, or the ability to speak or sleep. Women who internalize inflexible masculine ideals are likewise vulnerable to such gremlins.

I will offer a literary example of an adolescent in David Mitchell's semi-autobiographical novel *Black Swan Green*, as well as personal reflections of two analysts, Donald Moss and myself. Negotiation of masculinity can be particularly fraught in adolescence as variations from accepted norms can be severely punished by the group.

The concepts of 'masculinity' and 'femininity' are famously problematic. The experiences of masculinity, femininity and the complicated intermingling of these attributes are an ineluctable mixture of bodily, cultural, personally historic and intra-psychic factors. Masculinity is complex and can reside in boys or men in rigid or subtle forms – or more or less rigid/subtle forms – depending on different contexts or different relationships. Person points out: "[A] broad array of 'masculinities' exist, not only within different cultures, but also within any one culture" (2006: 1168). Likewise, Goldner describes a post-modern conception of "gender and sexuality as emerging in and through history and culture and thus . . . to be fluid and variable social categories" (2003: 114).

Reis argues that "male heterosexuality is not accorded the fluidity or multiplicity granted femininity or queer sexuality" (2009: 56) and advocates making room "for a multiplicity of masculine gendered representations" (2009: 56). But, as Harris describes Winnicott's view: "[G]ender is assumed to be fluid, but also crystallized, sometimes integrate-able and sometimes split and dissociated" (2016: 362). To acknowledge that there are rigidly held masculine ideals (as will be described by Corbett [2001] and Person [2006] in the next section of this chapter) is not to diminish the desire for more flexible options. In this chapter I will be considering a rigid view of masculine ideals that predisposes itself to splitting. I will first consider some gender theorists' ideas about masculine ideals and then offer several examples in order to reflect upon the symptoms that beset and attend it.

## Masculine Ideals

Corbett conceives of the ideal of masculinity as that of being a "big winner." He argues compellingly that "the wish and effort to be a big winner, not a small loser" (2001: 6) is a central male preoccupation:

> Many boys and men respond to the threat of smallness/losing with bravado and aggressive protest, which is often embodied through a kind of phallic intrusion/illusion: an insistent, illusory display of bigness and agency that is coupled with an equally unrestrained contempt for smallness and lack. In the spirit of 'boys will be boys,' bravado, aggressive protest, and illusory phallic narcissism have become defining, normative attributes of masculinity.
>
> (2001: 6)

Corbett considers boys' aggression as a way to conceal anxiety about losing, and reflects that boys' aggression is not adequately contained nor engaged by parents and society. He sees boys as left to rely on a "brittle bravado" and to over-rely on control and domination.

In a similar vein, Person sees "macho sexuality" as the Western cultural ideal for men.[1] She contends that "our culture sees male sexuality as domineering and even violent" (1986: 4), but she considers the wish to be in "control both of the sexual apparatus and of the partner" as more prevalent in men than are violent fantasies (1986: 6). Person describes males' emphasis on the power of the phallus and control of female (or male) partners as "at least in part compensatory anxieties engendered in the male developmental experience . . . an amalgam of castration anxiety, fear and envy of both sexes, and the fear (or experience) of loss of the object and loss of love" (1986: 6). She comments: "[T]he most striking feature of the male's sense of inadequacy is his belief that other men are truly in possession of macho sexuality. He feels macho sexuality is unobtainable for him personally, but not that it is a myth" (1986: 12).

In Corbett's and Person's views, the desires to be a big winner or to be macho sexually are invoked to preserve a precarious sense of self. Efforts to inhabit the masculine result in splitting off feelings of helplessness and dependence. However, the burden of unrelenting bigness creates masculinity as a kind of 'impossible profession,' leaving some men with a potential for split-off weakness, vulnerability and dependence to come crashing back in the form of capricious symptoms. Similarly, Dimen discusses gender in terms of splitting. She uses the concept of splitting "in its psychoanalytic sense both splitting of the ego and splitting of the object . . . and in its cultural sense the many dichotomies and dualisms paradigmatic in Western thinking . . . of critical relevance to feminist discourse" (1991: 336).

Excessive reliance on splitting and dissociation leaves us vulnerable to the precipitous return of disowned parts of ourselves. Split-off or dissociated parts of us have not benefitted from psychological work because they are disowned. When split-off or dissociated parts return, they do not come creeping in like, for example, a shift in mood. From a slightly different point of view, Corbett contends that men, in order to shore up their sense of masculinity, frequently use hatred and violence, including the projective term 'faggot' (2001: 24). Thus, the impossibility of incessant bigness necessitates extreme solutions: the bravado, hatefulness and aggression discussed by Corbett, or the splitting and potential intrusive return of a dissociated part of the self through gremlin-like symptoms discussed here.

One young man in analysis described to me his agonizing inability to attain an erection with his girlfriend or the seemingly inexplicable disappearance of an erection once attained. Although healthy, his first inclination was to understand his symptom as a medical problem, even though he had already consulted a urologist and no medical basis was found. He described his emotional experience upon penetrating a woman (or in fantasy, a man) as entering a dark, frightening place. Likewise, his experience of an inquiry into this problem (with me) also seemed like entering a dark and frightening place. Although this man was not hyper-masculine, his aversion to emotional meanings seemed to leave him in a traditionally male bind – unable to consider how his emotional experience affected his sexual functioning.

When anxiety is not too intense, we are more able to own and think about the troubled aspects of ourselves. But when the urgent necessity to meet a masculine ideal requires disowning major parts of ourselves, symptoms can come crashing back with an intrusive, trouble-making quality. Such 'mechanical failures' of erections, sleep or speech seem experientially captured by a gremlin, the *American Heritage Dictionary*'s first definition of which is "[A]n imaginary gnome-like creature to whom mechanical problems in aircraft are often attributed"; the second definition is "[A] mischief maker" (2017).

Conversely, femininity is often more ambivalently owned and thus less prey to collapse. The traditional feminine attributes of "pretty, passive, soft, docile, submissive, timid, compliant" (Elise, 1997: 491), seem more apologetically held to start with. Elise comments that it is questionable in society whether femininity is or is not something to aspire to. She describes femininity as a "[C]ulturally based term referring to a set of traits held in conflicted estimation – traits deemed socially desirable for females to express, yet not necessarily valued intrinsically" (1997: 491). Ironically, 'feminine' traits, which are less idealized in our culture, seem more stably held. 'Masculine' traits seem to acquire a sense of stability only if they are held in concert with other traits instead of in pure form.

Men are prey to reliance on splitting when unable to integrate weakness, need or gentleness with the masculine 'ideal.' Splitting leads to increasing idealization, in order to keep traditionally masculine attributes far away from attributes that are considered dangerously weak. Segal describes that "omnipotent denial may be used against excessive persecution . . . by idealizing the persecuting object itself, and treating it as ideal" (1964: 27). I believe this is the way some men experience masculinity. They feel persecuted by rigid ideals of masculine power, which are unattainable in their extremity, yet hold firmly to these ideals at the same time.

Mature integration of masculinity could involve the ability to discriminate between invigorating or exciting aspects of a masculine ideal and aspects that become too constraining or growth-inhibiting. Mature integration of masculinity could also involve tolerance of seemingly divergent qualities. I am reminded of Benjamin's (1988) embrace of multiple, contradictory selves that are characterized by gender fluidity and ambiguity. Dimen suggests that "[R]ecapturing split-off parts of the self therefore requires inhabiting its transitional spaces, including that in which gender is not a given but is in question" (1991: 335). The absence of such discrimination or fluidity was exemplified in a mid-adolescent boy I treated who told his father that he thought I wanted to make him into a girl, as I had asked him about his feelings. For this boy, the 'ideal' of masculinity involved a singled-minded focus on strength and athleticism, which allowed no inner world of feelings. This arrangement strangled the boy's development, as the simple experience or expression of emotion was profoundly threatening to his version of masculinity.

I will turn now to illustrations of capricious symptoms related to the ideal of masculinity.

## Boys and men

### A literary example

I offer the example of Jason, the 13-year-old protagonist in David Mitchell's 2006 semi-autobiographical novel *Black Swan Green*. The story is set in 1982 in Worcestershire, England. Jason is afflicted by a stammer that threatens everything for him – especially his already tentative place in the fierce hierarchy[2] of boys in his school. The stammer could lie dormant or unpredictably incapacitate him. The gremlin within could emasculate him with casual cruelty. Jason raises his hand to answer his teacher's question:

> The word 'nightingale' kaboomed in my skull but it just *wouldn't come out*. The n got out okay, but the harder I forced the rest the tighter the noose got. I remember Lucy Sneads whispering to Angela Bullock, stifling giggles. I remember Robin South staring at this bizarre sight. I'd've done the same if it hadn't been me. When a stammerer stammers their eyeballs pop out, they go trembly-red like an evenly matched arm wrestler, and their mouth guppergupperguppers like a fish in a net. It must be quite a funny sight. It wasn't funny for me though.
>
> (2006: 26)

Jason is a complex literary character and his stammer is multiply determined. His symptom can predominantly be seen in terms of conflicts regarding masculinity, but the author allows us to speculate about many possibilities. There is a secret in Jason's family that he seems to apprehend, yet not want to know. Does his stammer express the way truth in his family is strangled – to say it or not to say it? If the truth leads to the dismantling of the family, how can he speak? Yet, what is most starkly drawn in the book is a brutal hierarchy of early adolescent boys[3] – weakness is catastrophic and one's ranking in the caste system of boys is endlessly imperiled and easily lost.

Mitchell sets *Black Swan Green* in the macho England of Margaret Thatcher against the uneasy backdrop of the Falklands War. The so-called ideal of masculinity in a female is epitomized in Thatcher. Jason secretly wishes to be a poet – certain that if his peers were aware of this wish he would be permanently unmanned. His strangled speech implies a fear at revealing his 'effeminate' literary wishes and conversely the competitive dangers of his ambitious strivings. His parents are distracted by their own problems. He seems to live in a world of his own with no one to help him navigate his private fantasies in the external world. Without containing parents or parental figures, masculine ideals are particularly impossible. There is no one to stand for a type of strength that can include dependence or be inter-mingled with weakness.[4]

Winnicott's conception of maturational processes only occurring in a facilitating environment is relevant here. If father, or father in mother, can be experienced as strong, yet not afraid of some weakness, then there is greater likelihood that a livable version of masculinity can be imagined. The overwhelmed humiliation Jason experienced in his stammering is far more important than the words themselves. As Bion writes, for

> the stammerer . . . words, or lack of them, contain rather than communicate his meaning. Alternatively, the meaning is too powerful for the verbal formulation; the expression is lost in an 'explosion' in which the verbal formulation is destroyed.
>
> (1970: 194–195)

### Donald Moss: a childhood memory

Donald Moss has written a series of works on masculinity (2002, 2006, 2010, 2012), including a recent discussion of the impossibility of separating out identification and object love in masculine identity (2010). He asserts that to identify with a man is to love a man and that endless complications result. As a coda to this paper, Moss relates a boyhood memory of his own:

> In my first year of elementary school we were taught a new song each week. From the start, we were told that at the end of the year we would each be given a chance to lead the class in singing our favorite, which we were to keep secret . . . For me there was no doubt what my choice was going to be. The only song I loved was the lullaby 'When at Night I Go to Sleep' from *Hansel and Gretel* . . . [M]ine was, and would always be, the most beautiful song I had ever heard. This I knew. I sang it to myself every night. I'd always had trouble sleeping and easily went into a panic while lying in bed, imagining the disaster of never sleeping – days, weeks, months of it, and finally being sent away when it was decided that nothing could be done . . .
>
> It was late Spring when I got my chance to lead the class in singing for and about my angels . . . The teacher asked me what song I had chosen. I began to tell her: "It's the lullaby . . ." But immediately, out of the corner of my eye, I saw the reaction of the boys in the front row. Their faces were lighting up, in shock. They were looking at each other. Until then I hadn't even considered these boys, except for the certainty that my choice would surprise, that my secret had been kept intact.
>
> But, as I began to speak to the teacher, as I saw the faces of these boys, I knew, knew in a way that was immediate, clear and certain, that what I was about to do, the song I was about to choose, the declaration that I was about to make, represented an enormous and irrevocable error.
>
> (2010: 8–11)

The boyhood Moss perceived an enormous danger to his place with the boys if he exhibited little-boy longings and imaginative, aesthetic qualities. Moss' fear of crossing the unforgiving gaze of the boys recalls Jason's fear of the fierce hierarchy of early adolescent boys in his class. Moss' experience of sleep as capricious and unattainable recalls Jason's experience of speech as unreliable and unpredictable. The wish for an unassailable masculinity and fear of exclusion seemed to prevent Moss from softening into sleep (when he gave up his lullaby) or Jason from being able to participate in the inevitable imperfectability of speech. Both experienced their impotence in sleep or speech as a gremlin-like symptom, afflicting and preventing them from the idealized surface of masculinity. Their symptomatic inability to operate smoothly and without trouble (as is required in the masculine ideal) is in and of itself the return of the split-off and rejected uncertainty they did not want seen.

## Masculine ideals and gremlins within a woman

As is well known, Freud (1905, 1925, 1931) considered psychic bisexuality to be fundamental. He saw all people as having objects of identification who are both male and female and early love objects who are male and female. In this section I reflect upon a masculine ideal within a woman (myself). I am not intending to focus on women who are primarily identified with a masculine ideal, rather – what Ogden (1989) – calls the paradox of "masculinity in femininity." That is, how the internal object representation of father/maleness in the mother's unconscious is communicated to and internalized by her daughter.

Moss described a poignant memory of childhood insomnia, temporarily alleviated by the presence of the lullaby. The insomnia returned to him in gremlin-fashion when he forsook the lullaby in order to placate the boys in his class. His narration reminded me of the insomnia and capricious crises of confidence about public speaking that I experienced for several years. My confidence in sleeping or public speaking could evaporate unpredictably. Additionally, they were related – I might sleep poorly when I needed to speak in public and then feel less equipped to do so. My pleasure in sleeping or speaking publicly could mysteriously disappear. Jason's, Moss' and my experience is that of a gremlin afflicting us mysteriously and at will.

My gremlin-like symptoms strike me as connected with ideals of masculinity in myself. The image of a supremely confident, all-knowledgeable, public speaker – ready for any volley and impervious to criticism – is a traditional masculine ideal. Perhaps a feminine or bisexual self seems less equipped for the authoritative fray. Women who strive for such unobtainable and traditionally masculine ideals are vulnerable to gremlin-like symptoms.

Conflicts about performance can be understood in terms of castration anxiety, harsh superegos or anxieties about authority. Although over-familiar, these concepts are essential. However, I want to emphasize that the break-through of gremlin-like symptoms also has to do with the excessive nature of masculine ideals. No one is all-knowledgeable or without doubt.

My own version of the ideal of masculinity seems to me more connected to my mother's psychic life than to my father's. I, like all children, internalized both parents' ideals of masculinity, as well as broader cultural influences. My father was moderately successful, but also playful and relaxed with children. He seemed to inhabit a non-extreme version of masculinity with some self-doubt, but also some comfort. My mother envisioned a much more grand version of masculinity inspired by the Vatican. In her mind men were priests, bishops or ideally popes, and women worshipped and served them.[5] My father was unfortunately not a priest and so never seemed fully a man in my mother's eyes.

My mother's role would seem relegated to that of a supporting player – that of a woman in the Catholic Church. Yet, as Moss (2010) describes, object love and identification are inter-penetrative and so, in a sense, my mother was a priest. She felt superior to all who were not Catholic or deviated from any Catholic stricture, particularly regarding sexuality and certainly regarding homosexuality. And yet she also inhabited the feminine. She could be sweet, she cooked dinner and baked pies. When I was little, she read me stories and rocked me to sleep. I think that the gremlins afflicting my own public speaking have to do with the impossibilities of inhabiting a masculine ideal of authority – not just because it is impossible, but also because I miss my mother and my femaleness in it.

My mother's version of a masculine ideal is indeed extreme. Men are God and what they say is the Truth. The enticement in this view is obvious. Uncertainty is avoided. My mother's version of splitting left the degraded to the feminine and/or the homosexual. She could inhabit perfection through identification with men as God, and also inhabit an inferior female role. However, the female role was also more forgiving in that it was human. Not much was expected of women, but at least we could be human. When I ventured into 'the ideal of masculinity,' my symptomatic insomnia called me back to a version of myself in which perfection is impossible – made obvious in my inability to do the simplest thing – sleep. Perhaps we cannot go too far toward one love or one aspect of identification inside ourselves without threatening another. When I inhabit my version of my mother's extreme masculine ideal, I miss the feminine version of her and myself, i.e., the version that was denigrated and yet of more value than we knew.

The ability to integrate a masculine ideal is related in part to how extreme or moderated that ideal is. Parents are interpreters of culture. My mother's ideal[6] of men as God is impossible for anyone to inhabit and clearly prey to collapse. One could speculate that the male 'priestly' ideal she internalized was part of a larger cultural disaster: that of holding priests above the law and ignoring the protection of children in the pedophilia scandal in the Catholic Church – surely idealizing the so-called masculine and splitting off the weakness within those men. As Butler says:

> The more hyperbolic and defensive a masculine identification, the more fierce the ungrieved homosexual cathexis, and in this sense we might understand both 'masculinity' and 'femininity' as formed and consolidated through identifications that are composed in part of disavowed grief.
>
> (1995: 171)

## Conclusion

Clinically, the moment when a gremlin-like symptom sneaks through is a moment of potential opportunity. The disowned aspect has been unconsciously experienced as too horrifying, incompatible or unacceptable to be allowed a conscious lodging place. Accommodating these orphans is often a difficult psychological task in our patients and in our selves.

## Acknowledgments

First published as: Brady, M.T. (2017). Afflictions related to 'ideals' of masculinity: Gremlins within. *Contemporary Psychoanalysis, 53*(2): 196–208. Reprinted by permission of Taylor & Francis, LLC.

# Notes

1 Sarin (2012) notes that masculinity in Western cultures emphasizes the importance "of separation-individuation, autonomy, independence and initiative . . . and . . . identity conflicts in adolescence. In Asian cultures, such as those of India, Japan and possibly China and Korea, separation in childhood, as well as autonomy and initiative or even sharply differentiated images of self and other are considerably downplayed" (2012: 144).

2 Friedman and Downey describe certain boyhood characteristics of boys who will grow into the cultural norm for 'masculine': "In free play juvenile boys tend to be territorial, competitive, not accepting participation by girls and devaluing behaviors deemed feminine or girl-like. Verbalizations tend to be confrontational and replete with challenges, mockery and bravado" (2002: 209). Friedman and Downey comment that from early life, not only boys – but also grown men – tend to negatively categorize boys who do not match the cultural stereotype of masculinity.

3 Maccoby (1998) relates that taboos against cross-gender behavior tend to be enforced much more brutally by parents, peers and society generally when exhibited by boys.

4 Diamond (2009) notes that the boy who is able to achieve a reciprocal identification with an available, loving father who possesses a body and genitalia like his own is provided a foundation for a more secure and often more varied gendered expression of self.

5 Burkhalter, in a discussion of masculinity in South Africa, notes the "problematics of generalizing experience, and of reading this experience independent of the complexities and traumas of its accumulated history" (2016: 340). A cultural and religious institution with rigid and entrenched gender roles heavily affects my mother's version of masculinity. Likewise, Burkhalter notes that "gender roles in apartheid South Africa were largely considered distinct and evident, and dominant masculinities were held to be assumed and understood" (2016:342).

6 Parents' versions of the cultural ideals of masculinity or femininity are powerful but also internalized in relation to children's idiosyncratic fantasies.

# References

American Heritage Dictionary. (1982). *The American Heritage Dictionary of the English Language*, 2nd ed. Boston, MA: Houghton Mifflin Harcourt Publishing Company.

Benjamin, J. (1988). *The Bonds of Love*. New York: Random House.

Bion, W. (1970/1983). Attention and Interpretation. Oxford: Jason Aronson, pp 94–95.

Burkhalter, T. (2016). Foregrounding masculinities in psychoanalytic psychotherapy. *Psychoanalytic Dialogues, 26*: 339–351.

Butler, J. (1995). Melancholy gender – refused identification. *Psychoanalytic Dialogues*, *5*: 165–180.

Corbett, K. (2001). Faggot = loser. *Studies in Gender and Sexuality*, *2*(1): 3–28.

Diamond, M. (2009). Masculinity and its discontents: Making room for the mother inside the male – an essential achievement for healthy male gender identity. In *Heterosexual Masculinities and Contemporary Perspectives from Psychoanalytic Gender Theory*. New York: Routledge, pp. 23–54.

Dimen, M. (1991). Deconstructing difference: Gender, splitting, and transitional space. *Psychoanalytic Dialogues*, *1*: 335–352.

Elise, D. (1997). Primary femininity, bisexuality, and the female ego ideal: A re-examination of female developmental theory. *Psychoanalytic Quarterly*, *66*: 489–517.

Friedman, R., & Downey, J. (2002). *Sexual orientation and psychoanalysis: Sexual science and clinical practice*. New York: Columbia University Press.

Freud, S. (1905/1953). Three essays on the theory of sexuality. *Standard Edition, Vol. 7*. London: Hogarth Press.

Freud, S. (1925/1953). Some psychical consequences of the anatomical distinction between the sexes. *Standard Edition, Vol. 19*. London: Hogarth Press.

Freud, S. (1931/1953). Female sexuality. *Standard Edition, Vol. 21*. London: Hogarth Press.

Goldner, V. (2003). Ironic gender/authentic sex. *Studies in Gender and Sexuality*, *4*: 113–139.

Harris, A. (2016). Winnicott and gender madness. *British Journal of Psychotherapy*, *32*: 359–375.

Maccoby, E. (1998). *The Two Sexes: Growing Apart, Coming Together*. Cambridge, MA: Harvard University Press.

Mitchell, D. (2006). *Black Swan Green*. New York: Random House.

Moss, D. (2002). Internalized homophobia in men: Wanting in the first person singular, hating in the first person plural. *Psychoanalytic Quarterly*, *71*: 21–50.

Moss, D. (2006). Masculinity as masquerade. *Journal of the American Psychoanalytic Association*, *54*: 1187–1194.

Moss, D. (2010). Immaculate attachment vs. passive yearning: Thoughts on being and becoming a man. Unpublished paper given at a Scientific Meeting of the San Francisco Center for Psychoanalysis, San Francisco, CA.

Moss, D. (2012). *Thirteen Ways of Looking at a Man: Psychoanalysis and Masculinity*. New York, NY: Routledge.

Ogden, T.H. (1989). *The Primitive Edge of Experience*. Northvale, NJ: Jason Aronson.

Person, E. (1986). The omni-available woman and lesbian sex: Two fantasy themes and their relationship to the male developmental experience. In G. Fogel, F. Lane & R. Liebert (Eds.), *The Psychology of Men*. New York: Basic Books, pp. 71–94.

Person, E. (1986). Male sexuality and power. *Psychoanalytic Inquiry*, *6*: 3–25.

Person, E. (2006). Masculinities, plural. *Journal of the American Psychoanalytic Association*, *54*: 1165–1185.

Reis, B. (2009). Names of the father. In *Heterosexual Masculinities and Contemporary Perspectives from Psychoanalytic Gender Theory*. New York: Routledge, 55–72.

Sarin, M. (2012). The monks of Drepung Gomang Monastery: Impressions and speculation on alternative models of masculinity as they relate to resilience and trauma. *International Journal of Applied Psychoanalytic Studies*, *9*(2): 134–157.

Segal, H. (1964). *Introduction to the Work of Melanie Klein*. New York: Basic Books.

# Chapter 5

# Subversiveness in adolescence

'Amy,' age 15 and in her second year of analysis, imitates my manner after I greet her. I sit down, cross my legs and look expectant. She sits down, crosses her legs and looks expectant. I feel her skewering my comfortable conventions, but there is also something refreshing about it. An adult wouldn't do it – they might think, "Oh, this is canned," and might even say as much. But there is something distinctly adolescent about Amy's imitation of me. I think she is saying: "Why do you have these conventions?" In fact: "Why do all adults have their conventions?" As I reflected on Amy's satire of me I thought about the refreshingly radical quality in adolescent subversiveness.

In this chapter I will consider the subversive element of adolescence. The *American Heritage Dictionary* defines *subversive* as "intended or serving to subvert, esp. intended to overthrow or undermine an estab-lished government" (1982: 1214). In this sense, subversion is a task of adolescence – the younger generation must unseat the older one. Adolescent subversion can range from Amy's satiric challenging of my conventions to far more destructive overthrows. 'Rebelliousness' is often a characteristic ascribed to adolescents (Blos, 1967). Both *subver-sion* and *rebellion* refer to efforts to overthrow existing authority or governments. Subversion has a more covert and perhaps more intellec-tual and satiric quality than open and direct rebellion. Both are surely applicable to adolescence, but I find myself more intrigued with the quality of subversiveness, particularly in its potentially positive forms. Like *dissidence, subversion* seems to connote social critique more than the concept of *rebelliousness* does.

Subversion is part of what adolescents bring to the adult world – they see where we have become dulled or corrupt. For instance, 'Neil,' age 13, who came to analysis after his parents' divorce, says to me:

N:   My dad flirts with everyone.
A:   It is often hard for kids to see their parents start to have girlfriends or boyfriends after they are divorced, but it sounds like you are saying more than that.
N:   My dad's a pimp.
A:   How do you mean that?
N:   A pimp runs prostitutes.

While Neil was not able to say more at this point, his questioning of his father's narcissistic use of women would (over time) help him to consider his own internalization of some of his father's feelings toward females (which I will discuss further below).

Subversiveness is a complex state as it wavers on an edge between liveliness and aggression or even violence. Adolescence without some sort of subversiveness just couldn't be adolescence. Subversiveness is also a rich concept in that it has theoretical status in many disciplines, such as Social Theory (Marcuse, 1964, 1965/1969; Adorno, 1991), Feminist Theory and Queer Theory[1] (Butler, 1990) and Literary Criticism[2] (Lurie, 1990; Remigio, 2008; Saxena, 2012). It connects personal feeling, familial dynamics, power structures and political-cultural critique. The adolescent developmental task of questioning the status quo can contribute to the development of our capacities to question ourselves and the world around us in adulthood.

True subversiveness involves a genuinely questioning dimension, as distinguished from a superficial adoption of a style. I think this was true for Amy. She had many reasons to be disillusioned with adults and to question how we did things. Her parents had a veneer of wealth and social prominence. Underneath this, Amy could see her father's depressive collapse and her mother's shallow partying. Amy played out her anger at her parents through provocations such as unauthorized piercings and minor criminal activity (graffiti and shoplifting). Over time her angry critique of the older generation seemed to help her to separate from the serious problems of her parents.

I could view Amy's symptoms as the "anti-social tendency" described by Winnicott (1958). He describes a

> mixture of stealing and hurting and messing . . . *the nuisance value of the anti-social child is an essential feature*, and is also, at its best, *a favourable feature* indicating again a potentiality for recovery of lost fusion of the libidinal and motility drives.
>
> (1958: 311)

Winnicott's conception of the anti-social tendency captures something about Amy – the mixture of her deprivation of true parental care, her angry 'messing,' and her (largely unconscious) effort to force the environment to respond. What I am trying to add here is that there was also an element of social critique. She was clearly struggling with the corruption and dysfunction she rightly saw in the older generation and was in a sense saying to us (often in provocative action), "You make up these rules and choose to follow whichever are convenient to you – I reject your efforts to make me superficially conform to what is comfortable for you."

## Digression

At 23, barely more than an adolescent myself, I entered a doctoral program in Clinical Psychology at the Wright Institute in Berkeley. Mystified by my older classmates' commentary on Lacan and Foucault, I was also adjusting to unconventional Berkeley after an Irish Catholic upbringing in New England. The Wright Institute was a heady place at the time, foregrounding the interface of psychoanalysis with Social Theory. The atmosphere of intellectualism and subversive questioning owed a great deal to its birth. Its founder Nevitt Sanford had been a professor of psychology at the University of California at Berkeley. In 1950, Berkeley dismissed him (and 11 other professors) because of their refusal to sign the draconian loyalty oath required of them by the university during the McCarthy era.[3]

Sanford launched the Wright Institute in 1968. In the intervening years, he was a critic of the over-emphasis on academic publishing in evaluating professors, which he saw as leading to deterioration in teaching abilities. Sanford was also an early critic of IQ tests, saying they were biased in favor of the white middle class. He was a champion of making college more accessible to minority students.

Sanford is best known for his co-authorship of *The Authoritarian Personality* (1950) with two refugees from Nazism, Theodor Adorno and Else Frenkel-Brunswik, and Daniel Levenson. The book is a study of fascism and anti-Semitism. The purpose of their work was to understand the vulnerability to fascistic leadership and anti-Semitism that had occurred under Hitler, Mussolini, and others. *The Authoritarian Personality* proposes that a set of personality traits termed the 'F scale' (fascism scale) cluster together based on childhood experience. These traits include conventionalism, authoritarian submission/aggression, anti-intellectualism and superstition. Their research showed that those prejudiced against one racial, religious, or ethnic group were likely to be prejudiced against others (Goleman, 1995). This study melded a psychoanalytic understanding of development with interrelated social forces.[4]

Thus, the Wright Institute was heir to Sanford's subversive refusal to sign the loyalty oath (which undermined intellectual and political freedom), as well as to his concern (noted in Sanford's obituary by Peter Dybwad, president of the Wright) "that graduate schools had become too narrow in their thinking, the problems they approached, and their student body" (Goleman, 1995).

Social Theory lends a meaningful addition to developmental or psychoanalytic thought regarding subversion. For instance, the philosopher and social theorist Herbert Marcuse (1965/1969) suggests that mass culture, with its profusion of consumerism and sexual provocations, serves to reinforce political repression. Political energy for constructive change is drained away if people are preoccupied with consumption and inauthentic sexual stimulation. Thus, a seemingly free or permissive internal or external culture may remain quite uncritical of existing forces. In a similar vein, the philosopher and sociologist Theodor Adorno (1991) describes a "culture industry" of popular music and artistic forms which he sees as having a mind-numbing quality that diminishes the transgressive potentials of art.

Growing up within the orthodoxies of Catholic grammar and high schools my own capacity for subversion emerged only once I started college at 17. Feminism, communism and theologies of liberation were all important aspects of my Jesuit education at the College of the Holy Cross. While misogyny and cultural narrowness were aspects of my experience there, intellectual questioning was quite free. Like Sanford's McCarthy-era experience, there was much for me to question in the heartland of the American Catholic Church (during a time that would later be known as the height of the Catholic Church's ignoring, or what might better be called facilitating, pedophile priests).

An independent sense of self and a reflective, questioning attitude toward received orthodoxies in educational, social and political spheres has roots in the adolescent process. Oppressive or corrupt leadership in an academic or political setting highlights the positive elements of subversion.

## Generational overthrow

Within psychoanalysis, Loewald (1980), in particular, captures the transfer of power from one generation to the next. In the process adolescents struggle with guilt at their effort to overthrow or more quietly subvert. Parents struggle with – and sometimes resist – the passage of generations.

From an ego psychological perspective, Blos (1967) describes a new organization of the personality in adolescence arising through testing of the self by going to excess, oppositional attitudes, rebellious behavior and resistive strivings. But, while I agree that adolescence necessitates a "second individuation process" (Blos, 1967), my interest in the concept of subversion is that it captures the interpersonal and structural forces (as I discuss in Chapter 3) at work in the passage of generations. In adolescence, internal and external object relations are in profound tension.

In order for the adolescent to attain adulthood, there must be a shift in the generations. Loewald (1980) says this involves, in some sense, the murder of the parents. As I discuss in Chapter 3, the psychological murder of the parents is one critical aspect, but only one aspect, of the problem of the passage of generations. In the arduous process of development adolescents want to kill their parents *and* keep them alive. The adolescent splits off his need to murder the older generation from his love for his parents. In splitting off aggressive parts they are less integrated and feel potentially more dangerous.

Gaines (1999), an interpersonal theorist, describes a "re-negotiation" that occurs in adolescence and critiques an over-emphasis on separation in psychoanalytic theory. I certainly agree that a renegotiation occurs, but would not want to minimize the intense unconscious elements at work as the body is changing and the demands of adulthood are in sight.

I will relate two vignettes of 'Evelyn,' an adolescent in analysis, to convey unconscious elements that underlie adolescents' renegotiation with their parents and the world. Here is a dream from when Evelyn is 16 and has her first serious boyfriend:

*E:*  The dream was so awful. I was in a gloomy home in a dark wood. I was supposed to have killed someone. The woman lying on the bed had been stabbed but was alive. I assumed I killed her. I put tape around her eyes and mouth. I felt the woman was me, but I killed her. Someone picks me up and I had blood all over me. I was in jail and was confused. I felt very guilty about what I did. If I got out of jail I would go to hell. If I repent I could forgive myself. I couldn't escape this heavy guilt. Being in jail was the best place for me because there I wouldn't have to deal with society or my family. I felt comfortable in jail. At the same time, I was thinking of ways of getting out. It felt so real. I woke up and thought, "Thank God it's not true." At dinner last night my dad talked about how when he was a little boy he almost witnessed his uncle shooting his aunt. I couldn't believe my dad didn't go into treatment. He was eight or nine. I would have gone nuts. I would die. No wonder my dad has a hard time being aggressive. He said he ran into the kitchen and almost ran my aunt over. He saw her lying on the floor. In the dream I didn't see myself stab the woman, but I was taping her mouth and eyes. Covering with duct tape. I have difficulty saying what I think. I don't know …

*A:*  You were saying what you think, but then trailed off.

*E:*  I have difficulty using my brain. When I'm with my boyfriend I have trouble looking into his eyes and kissing him too. It's like killing, death. In the dream she was bleeding but alive. How could you be alive when someone stabbed you a million times?

*A:*  Stabbing is a particular way of killing someone. You seem very afraid about your boyfriend entering your eyes and mouth.

*E:*  And my heart too, the woman was stabbed in that area, in the middle.

Evelyn said that she feared her boyfriend's preoccupation with her might hurt him, as he was neglecting his responsibilities. Evelyn wished for and was afraid of her boyfriend penetrating her, both physically and emotionally. In the intensity of their physical passion she felt taken over by him, and in that way killed off. Simultaneously, her new physical experience can be understood as killing off childhood parts of her self and killing off the place her mother had with her.

Adolescents need their parents, but it is in a different way than before. It is important for Evelyn's parents to be close to her in creating 'brakes' that she could use so that she would not have to turn to the superego 'jail' withdrawal and punishment state. Close parents can also communicate in myriad subtle ways that they accept their adolescent's sexual development, that they have survived these transitions themselves and that their developing teen will too.

Two years later, now 18, Evelyn decides, for the first time, not to go away on vacation with her family. Although she makes the decision, her vituperation is noteworthy:

*E:* I hate my mother – you don't even know how much I can't stand her. I hate my father's side of the family and my mother's side. My aunt gets medication for depression and doesn't take it. My mother refuses to do anything. They're all fucking spoiled brats. My father's a lazy ass who thinks religion is going to save him from turmoil. They all look to me as if I'm supposed to save the family from falling apart and I can't do that. My mom has the nerve to make me feel guilty for coming here, that they could use the money for C. (her brother). They can die on their vacation for all I care. All of a sudden I'm hating my grandmother too. I just feel like killing everyone off.

Evelyn is a prized child to both parents. Her mother has separation difficulties of her own and undermines Evelyn's development of appropriate responsibility and autonomy as well as her relationship with anyone outside the family. Evelyn's subversive critique of her family is allowing her to develop her own mind and her own views. Simultaneously, this vignette also captures the splitting of loving and hateful feelings that the adolescent process involves. Evelyn was in a rage at her family's departure and her increasing independence. She has real reasons to be angry at her mother, but also loves her intensely. She can more easily leave her childhood family if they seem devoid of value.

Teens in treatment often solicit analysts to play out parental roles, particularly when parents are insufficiently psychically present for the adolescent to struggle with. Winnicott suggests: "[I]f parent-figures abdicate, then the adolescents must make a jump to a false maturity and lose their greatest asset: freedom to have ideas and act on impulse" (1971: 150). If provocation or subversiveness can meet with genuine engagement by parents or analysts there is a chance of growth. For instance, Amy (mentioned above) had been telling me about her sneaking out of her house at night to do graffiti. I noticed a small 'tag' on a wall in my office hallway and thought this might be her work. I asked her if she had done it, and while she acknowledged she had, she said: "You are making a big deal out of nothing." I replied: "You didn't tell me you did it and by having a secret from me you remove yourself from our relationship. I think your secretiveness also contributes to distance from your mother. You and your mom seem to be drifting apart. When you told her about your marijuana use it was hard, but at least you were engaged with each other."

Adolescent subversion might result in thoughtful or honest responses from adults – where we are able to acknowledge our conventions or follies, yet hold to the 'governance' necessary for our adolescents' well-being. Ideally, in pushing up against an adult, the adolescent gets a reaction and simultaneously reassures her or himself about the solidity of the object.

On the other hand, at times adolescent subversion only reveals the incapacity of adults in the environment to respond. In this case, the 'established government' is not really trustworthy (at least in some areas) and so there is real trouble. Even in the best of situations, the adolescent's need to overthrow the established government in order to claim her or his own capacities is a fraught endeavor.

In Chapter 3 I discuss succession problems for both the adolescent and the parent. Subversion is an important aspect of the adolescent side of this process. The adult part involves some mixture of legitimate authority, repressive or oppressive forces and whatever level of willingness or unwillingness we have to gradually cede the center of gravity to the next generation.

Analysts widely view adolescence as a period when oedipal struggles are reengaged with a body now capable of full sexuality, murder and suicide (Anderson, 2005; Nicolo, 2015). I put this starkly because some adolescents do die in this process. An adolescent comes to mind who felt the only way out of her rage at an oppressive mother was through suicide. Loewald (1980) conveys that there is a necessary element of death in the adolescent process. Generational change does involve the overthrow of a generation:

[I]n our role as children of our parents, by genuine emancipation we do kill something vital in them – not all in one blow and not in all respects, but contributing to their dying. As parents of our children we undergo the same fate, unless we diminish them. If eventually some sort of balance, equality, or transcending conciliation is achieved, children and parents are fortunate.

(Loewald, 1980: 395)

There is a spectrum of adolescent subversiveness. At one end is a sort of non-violent overthrow. 'Luke,' a late adolescent in analysis, told me about a weekend at his family's beach house accompanied by his friends instead of his parents. This excursion included some experimental drug use. Clearly there was a quality of anticipatory identification – "What would it be like to be independent and not have to rely on parents?" While there can be a somewhat manic quality to such experimentation, this incident did not seem overly destructive. Luke could imagine being without his parents, but his parents were still in contact emotionally. Similarly, in the transference he seemed to partially provoke me into questioning his judg-ment (re the drug use) but also to engage with me in telling me the story. I realize as I relate this vignette, however, that the 'non-violent overthrow' sense of this incident is partly due to the fact that there were no major adverse consequences of the weekend. With adolescents it often feels like there is an element of chance about this. There are adolescent parties in which safety or disaster might be the likely outcomes, but a substantial element of luck is often at play.

At the other end of the spectrum is a darker version of subversiveness. In this case the adolescent may need to be stopped from an overthrow of adult governance they are not ready for. I was concerned about Neil, who was now 15, and his escalating substance abuse.[5] He told me of excessive alcohol and drug use, including MDMA and cocaine. In our sessions, I felt that he tied my hands to any real consideration of the risks he was taking. One day he told me of having vomited in his sleep after having blacked out from drinking the night before. I told him that he could have died if he had choked on his vomit while blacked out. I said that we needed to meet with his parents to tell them what was hap-pening, and that I would prefer he tell them, but that if he could not, then I would. He started to bargain to not be removed from too much of his daily life, but he did not challenge my drawing a line about getting sober and getting additional intensive out-patient substance abuse treatment along with his analysis. For Neil, legitimate parental authority needed to take hold before subversion could be creative.

What could look like reckless rebelliousness and indifference to adult authority in this boy (he had frequently denied the danger of his escalating substance abuse) was really a desperate cry for parental functioning. Here, subversion of parental authority – e.g., "I will do whatever I want and I don't care what you think" – needed to be given some room, but at a critical point it also required timely adult intervention. Neil could see that I was not just trying to keep him a child, as I only intervened when provocation, rebellion and subversion reached life-threatening proportions.

Such cases of dangerous rebellion and subversion throw the analyst and the parents into a state of struggle with the adolescent. I had been contending with how to respond to this Neil's recklessness for some time, and, at the point mentioned above, my concern reached a new level. While clearly Neil could disown his own concern for his life, he was also lodging it with me, so that someone could be engaged with his survival. Such examples of disturbing subversiveness may be preferable to an adolescent feeling there is not someone involved enough to be disturbed. These are adolescents whose parents are so preoccupied, absent or troubled that there seems no chance of getting through. In this way subversion implies a relationship to the 'established government,' however hostile it may be.

There is a profound interface and subversion for adolescents between the individual and the group. One's pre-existing relationship to the group (family) is subverted. The adolescent forsakes, in part, her or his role within the group (family) and yet urgently seeks a new role in a new group (peers).[6] Developing individuality is counter-balanced by often extreme conformity to the new group – as dependency is shifted onto this new arrangement. The new group is hostile to further individuation, even though joining it in the first place was an effort to individuate. For instance, I have often heard of pressure exerted by members of a group on a member who has changed in some way (e.g., is no longer using drugs through work in the treatment). Change in one individual in the group can threaten the group's denial of its problems – such as the promotion of escalating substance abuse.

Adolescents in treatment often play out these issues in visceral ways. The adolescent may join with the analyst (in opposition to the parents), or may reject the analyst, in part or in whole, in favor of membership in a new group. I am reminded of Loewald's description that the parents (and I would add the analyst) are destroyed in adolescence:

> In the process of becoming and being an adult, significant emotional ties with parents are severed. They are not simply renounced . . . but they are also actively rejected, fought against, and destroyed to varying degrees. Perhaps this active rejection represents a 'change of function,' a form of taking over actively what had to be endured passively in the beginning. Be that as it may, in the course of what we consider as healthy development this active urge for emancipation comes to the fore.
>
> (1980: 388–389)

## Adolescent Subversion – Pre and Post

In order to put adolescent subversion in perspective, I offer a few ideas about what comes before and after adolescent subversion. A paper entitled 'Jump-rope rhymes and the rhythm of latency development in girls' (Goldings, 1974) captures the essence of latency for me. Goldings quotes jump-rope rhymes replete with sex, aggression and death. The rhythms and rules of the jump-rope rhymes organize, submerge and allow for this freedom of expression so that sex and aggression can be elaborated and contained for now. Here are two examples:

> I had a little brother
> His name was Tiny Tim
> I put him in the washtub
> To teach him how to swim
> He drank up all the water
> Ate up all the soap
> He died last night
> With a bubble in his throat
>
> (Goldings, 1974: 438)

Or:

> Cinderella
> Dressed in yella
> Went upstairs

To kiss her fella
By mistake
She kissed a snake
How many doctors
Did it take?

(Goldings, 1974: 444)

In a similar vein, 'Adele,' a 10-year-old girl in twice-weekly psychotherapy, has carefully constructed a 'romance game' with me. Cards are drawn
that progress the player in the game: 'You go to prom,' 'You get engaged,'
'You have twins,' etc. Likewise, cards can be drawn that send one back-
ward in the game, such as 'You get divorced.' The excitement and dangers
of romance are clearly on Adele's mind, but her desire to follow rules is
palpably present. She is excited about romance and fearful of missteps,
but there is not yet a familial, social or cultural critique here. Adele does
not want to break a rule or make a mistake.

Without some prior latency structure, adolescent subversion might be
more like chaos or disorganization. Subversion allows for the elaboration
of increasingly individual thought if some capacity for order and containment has developed.

After adolescence, subversion ideally takes on more secondary process
thought (e.g., Sanford's cultural critiques described above). Neil's angry
comment that his father "is a pimp" was a step toward independent observation, but a long way from more elaborated and integrated thought. Neil
returned to treatment at 22, five years after the end of his first analysis.
During that second period he grappled with lying to and cheating on his
girlfriend. Gradually, he was able to question his unwillingness to grant a
woman a clear role with him. His adolescent subversive critique of his
father ultimately contributed to a more adult capacity to question himself
as well as others.

The liveliness of an adolescent part of the personality in adults also
includes productive subversion – skepticism of the status quo in oneself
and one's surroundings. The analyst's ability to tolerate a vital adolescent
part of herself or himself is crucial to facilitating patients' elaboration of
these experiences.

In discussing any concept we run the risk of over-simplification.
Here, I am mainly discussing the positive aspects of subversion. When
we examine clinical material in detail this point of view begins to fray.

An incident with Neil comes to mind during my work with him as an adult. Reticent to anger in the outside world, Neil argued that his sado-masochistic activities with his girlfriend did not merit questioning on my part, as – after all – they were adult and consensual. The capacity to feel and pursue one's sexual interests is crucial. What would sexuality be if it didn't include this wild and subversive element of one's own desires? However, I found myself uneasy as Neil told me of his activities with his girlfriend. Though adult, she is younger than Neil. When he told me of slapping her during sex to the point of bruising her, I told him I thought he should stop it. I am aware some analysts might have inter-vened sooner and others would not have said what I did.

Neil's capacity to question received dictums is important. In Chapter 2 I wrote about the dangers of analysts inflicting cultural normativities. At the same time, I felt I could not stand by while Neil hurt his girlfriend. After my intervention Neil became concerned about my regard for him. I told him that I could still appreciate him and simultaneously think that hurting his girlfriend was not a good idea.

## Conclusion

The social theorist Marcuse (1965/1969) suggests: "[S]urely, no govern-ment can be expected to foster its own subversion, but in a democracy such a right is vested in the people (i.e., in the majority of the people)." Likewise, as analysts and parents we can't be expected to foster our own subversion, and hopefully can carry the need to be an established gov-ernment until such time as an adolescent is more ready to take on her or his own governance. But, just as in a democracy, this process is any-thing but smooth. Subversion and separation can be full of irrational forces for both the established government (parents) and the people (adolescents).

Adolescents challenge our comfortable equilibrium. Subversion is not unique to adolescents in treatment, but analysts and therapists of adoles-cents particularly need to move around in the prickly experience of being subverted. In her final session, 'Rachel,' a late adolescent, gave me a small cactus to convey that she knew how prickly she had been with me. I am left with a cactus and a sense of gratitude for the authenticity of Rachel's interactions with me – including her questioning why our being together would have any meaning or value.

## Acknowledgment

First published as Brady, M.T. (2017). Subversiveness in adolescence. *Contemporary Psychoanalysis, 53*(3), pp. 346–361.

## Notes

1 Butler sees gender as a kind of improvised performance, a form of theatricality that constitutes a sense of identity. She contends that if the appearance of gender is an effect of culturally influenced acts, then no solid universal gender exists. Butler calls for subversive action – for people to trouble the categories of gender through performance.
2 Lurie (1990), for instance, argues that all great children's literature is subversive in that the characters gain an independence of and mock pompous adults. Saxena (2012) contends that while the Harry Potter series is very much within the epic hero tradition, elements of the series ultimately question and undermine mainstream values. She sees Hogwarts as a liminal territory, home to magic and "queering" forces where marginalized characters and unconventional relationships are safeguarded – as a fantastical space that subverts the traditional masculine and heterosexual agenda of a heroic epic.
3 A decision by the California Supreme Court in 1959 resulted in Sanford's reinstatement at UC Berkeley. He left UC Berkeley for Stanford in 1961 and left Stanford to found the Wright Institute in 1968.
4 Taub (2016) discusses the question of why large numbers of people can rapidly adopt extreme political views that seem to coincide with a fear of minorities and the desire for a strongman leader. She examines why the Republican electorate has supported as extreme a candidate as Donald Trump, and notes that what makes it even more puzzling is that his supporters cross demographic lines. Research (MacWilliams, 2016a, 2016b) indicates that not only does authoritarianism (a psychological profile of individuals characterized by a desire for order and fear of outsiders) correlate with Trump support, but also it does so more reliably than virtually any other indicator. Hetherington and Weiler (2009) note that demographic and economic changes such as immigration "activated" authoritarian tendencies, leading many Americans to seek a strongman leader who would preserve a status quo they feel is under threat.
5 This patient has been discussed at greater length in Brady (2016).
6 See Chapter 7 for a discussion of family and group forces in adolescence.

## References

Adorno, T., Frenkel-Brunswik, E., Levinson, D., & Sanford, N. (1950). *The Authoritarian Personality*. New York: Harper and Row.
Adorno, T. (1991). *The Culture Industry*. London: Routledge.

American Heritage Dictionary. (1982). *The American Heritage Dictionary of the English Language*, 2nd ed. Boston, MA: Houghton Mifflin Harcourt Publishing Company.

Anderson, R. (2005). Adolescence and the body ego: The reencountering of primitive mental functioning in adolescent development. *Unpublished paper presented at the Sixteenth Annual Melanie Klein Memorial Lectureship*, January 8, 2005, Los Angeles, CA.

Blos, P. (1967). The second individuation process. *Psychoanalytic Study of the Child, 22*: 162–186.

Brady, M.T. (2016). Substance abuse in an adolescent boy: Waking the object. In *The Body in Adolescence: Psychic Isolation and Physical Symptoms*. London: Routledge: pp. 57–73.

Butler, J. (1990). *Gender Trouble: Feminism and the Subversion of Identity*. New York: Routledge.

Gaines, R. (1999). The interpersonal matrix of adolescent development and treatment. In A. Esman (Ed.), *Adolescent Psychiatry, 24*. New York: Routledge, pp. 25–47.

Goldings, H.J. (1974). Jump-rope rhymes and the rhythm of latency development in girls. *Psychoanalytic Study of the Child, 29*: 431–450.

Goleman, D. (1995). Nevitt Sanford, 86, psychologist who traced roots of prejudice. *New York Times*, July 11.

Hetherington, M., & Weiler, J. (2009). *Authoritarianism and Polarization in American Politics*. New York: Cambridge University Press.

Loewald, H. (1980). The waning of the Oedipus complex. In *Papers on Psychoanalysis*. New Haven, CT: Yale University Press, pp. 384–404.

Lurie, A. (1990). *Don't Tell the Grown-Ups: The Subversive Power of Children's Literature*. Boston, MA: Little, Brown and Company.

MacWilliams, M. (2016a). www.politico.com/magazine/story/2016/01/donald-trump-2016-authoritarianism-213533

MacWilliams, M. (2016b). www.vox.com/2016/2/23/11099644/trump-support-authoritarianism

Marcuse, H. (1964). *One-Dimensional Man: Studies in Ideology of Advanced Industrial Society*. London: Routledge.

Marcuse, H. (1965/1969). Repressive tolerance. In Wolff, R., Moore, B., & Marcuse, H. *A Critique of Pure Tolerance*. Boston, MA: Beacon Press.

Marohn, R. (1998). A reexamination of Peter Blos's concept of prolonged adolescence. In A. Esman (Ed.), *Adolescent Psychiatry, 23*. Hillsdale, NJ: Analytic Press, pp. 3–19.

Nicolo, A. (2015). Psychotic functioning in adolescence: The perverse solution to survive. *International Journal of Psychoanalysis, 96*: 1335–1353.

Remigio, M. (2008). Adolescent empires: Identity, liminality, and advocacy in contemporary American literature. *George Washington University doctoral dissertation*. Retrieved from ProQuest Dissertations Publishing. (3297028)

Saxena, V. (2012). *The Subversive Harry Potter: Adolescent Rebellion and Containment in the J.K. Rowling Novels*. Jefferson, NC: McFarland.

Taub, A. (2016). www.vox.com/2016/3/1/11127424/trump-authoritarianism

Winnicott, D.W. (1958). The anti-social tendency. In D.W. Winnicott (Ed.), *Through Paediatrics to Psycho-Analysis*. New York: Basic Books, pp. 306–315.

Winnicott, D.W. (1971). *Playing and Reality*. New York: Basic Books.

# Chapter 6

# 'Thinking under fire'

## Bionian concepts in the treatment of adolescents and children

Bion did not treat adolescents or younger children, yet many of his inter-related concepts, such as container/contained, maternal reverie and the development of thinking through alpha function, are highly applicable to their treatment. Additionally, his conceptualizations of thinking and non-thinking states (K or -K links) underlie the possibility for development in children and adolescents, that is, of 'learning from experience.' Bion's premise that the purpose of analysis is the growth of the mind is synony-mous with the child or adolescent analyst's goals of fostering development and understanding impediments to development.

This chapter will consider these concepts and then explicate them through the descriptions of two psychotherapies: one of a child and one of an adolescent.

Bion views child analysis as 'extremely creative' in releasing capacities because the defenses of children are less fossilized than those of adults (2005: 55).[1] In *The Tavistock Seminars*, Bion comments:

> [P]eople say, "It's no good to psychoanalyse a child of two or three or five." I have even heard fantastic statements about not being able to do anything when "the fibres are not myelinated". The trouble with the myelinated fibres is that the person who has them is often so rigid, so structured, that you can't get another idea through their myelin.
>
> (2005: 15)

Bion describes real contact between any two people as like a storm – capturing how unsettling it is to sense that the other person in the consulting room is completely different from oneself. For adults treating children or adolescents, an added level of the foreign intensifies the storm. Ogden says that in order to read early Bion, "the reader must be able to tolerate not knowing, getting lost, being confused and pressing ahead anyway" (2004a: 286). This uncertain state of mind is analogous to what a child or adolescent therapist needs to sustain. Even more than with adult patients, we can lose our bearings. There is less secondary process thought. There is less of the veneer of social conventions. There is more action and, often, more commotion: the adolescent girl refuses to come into the building for her session; the adolescent boy comes high to his session; the teenager's parents call to say she organized a party where Ecstasy was taken. Adolescent sexuality, in its palpable quality, can also feel like a storm to an adult. In all of us sexuality can feel like contact with a primal, hot, stormy force – but even more so in the adolescent and the adults involved with him or her.

Bion (1970) emphasizes the differences between thinking about an experience and being in an experience. Psychoanalytic treatment of children immerses us in a dream scene brought to life in play, art, imaginary roles, action and words. Psychoanalytic treatment of adolescents immerses us in a dream scene brought to life in acting out, acting in, words and (for many teens) drawing or music. With a profound respect for the difficulty of thinking under pressure and an appreciation for our need for containment in order to be able to think, Bion says that we need to be able to 'interpret under fire.' The analyst of a child or adolescent is under fire much of the time. We must participate in play and react to behavior, absorbing the feelings and roles conveyed in the analytic field. We must react to behavior inside and outside of sessions, particularly with adolescents. At times we might need to confront and set limits, while struggling to retain our capacity to think.

Bion was heavily influenced by his experiences in the First World War, which he entered in his own late adolescence, at age 19. The devastation of combat affected him for a lifetime. Additionally, his first wife died in childbirth. After he married his second wife, Francesca, Bion had a remarkably fertile period of writing, during which he developed many of his seminal ideas such as container/contained, a theory of thinking and attacks on linking. This foment of theoretical development seems related in part to the safety his relationship with his wife accorded him, allowing his return to the horror of his war experience (Brown, 2012). In his own life, his personal experience of trauma, the painful difficulty of growth and the containment that made it possible captures the essence of Bion's thinking.

I will briefly consider Bion's inter-related concepts of maternal reverie and container/contained in relation to the development of thinking. I will then focus on the K link as a key to understanding the clinical material of a 7-year-old girl and then of a 16-year-old girl. Bion's relationship to theory is unique in that while he acknowledges its importance in allowing us to see something in a new way, he also says that we must be ready to discard theory as it can offer a false sense of understanding: "[A]s we try to express or formulate our findings . . . so we also excrete a kind of shell around them, a layer of knowledge that we can neither penetrate nor break out of" (2005: 33).

## The development of thinking

Bion sees the first form of thinking as striving to know another emotionally. Early emotional events between a mother[2] and her infant are decisive for the capacity to think in the infant and for the possibility of growth in the mother. Bion sees thinking as a human link, as the emotional experience of trying to know oneself or another.

As is well known, Bion expanded Klein's concept of projective identification beyond its defensive uses. Klein saw projective identification as a necessary developmental step in early childhood, along with splitting, to separate dangerous, hostile impulses from loving ones (Klein, 1975). That is, the badness or anxiety too difficult to experience inside the self is evacuated out into the other – sometimes by an adolescent in the form of provocative action or aggression. Bion acknowledged Klein for her insights into projective identification, but also took the concept in an expansive, new direction. He saw projective identification as not just a mechanism of defense, but as the first mode of communication between mother and infant – as the first rudiment of thinking.

The infant conveys his fears to his mother by projecting them into her for her to receive and know. The mother receives the fears and thinks about them, struggling to contain them by giving them meaning. The mother then conveys the results of her struggles and thinking by projecting them back into the infant, who introjects her metabolized thinking. Thus, the child's gradual ability to know him or herself is facilitated by being taken in and known in his mother's mind. As adolescent therapists, we are also concerned about the support and containment that parents have or lack, as well as their internal capacities for containment.

Parents are pressed hard to absorb the extreme feelings of adolescents. In the next chapter, I will discuss a Bionian approach to parent work in analytic treatment with adolescents.

## Maternal reverie

According to Bion, maternal reverie is the capacity of the primary object to love and think about his or her infant, allowing the infant gradually to internalize a parent who is able to think and, optimally, to absorb the experience that his or her feelings can be modified, understood and related to. Patients who have experienced little maternal reverie convey (in words or actions) that they experience their feelings as uncontestable 'facts.' In treatment, the therapist receives these raw, unmodulated feelings through projective identification. Bion writes: "[I]f the feeding mother cannot allow reverie or if the reverie is allowed but is not associated with love for the child or its father this fact will be communicated to the infant even though incomprehensible to the infant" (1962: 36). This lack of the experience of reverie leaves the infant without the sense that experiences can be thought about or that pain and frustration can be ameliorated by love.

The analyst's reverie is, ideally, grounded in a state of mind as open as possible to experiencing what is most true for the patient, and then finding words to convey something of that truth back to the patient. Some form of transformation in playing, dreaming or thinking is only possible when the analyst takes the patient's experience in at a depth. Bion saw this as an endlessly courageous and creative state – the willingness to know another person, at which we are always partially failing – but pressing ahead anyway.

## Container/contained

Bion sees the personality as constituted by two elements – contained and container – in a dynamic intercourse or relationship, with the contained continually seeking a container. Symington and Symington (1996: 52) say, "The archetype for container/contained is mother's breast/infant." In an attuned relationship between a mother and baby, a sense of a loving relationship can be internalized into the infant's personality, which transforms into an internal healthy container and contained dynamic in the infant. Alternatively, in a misattuned relationship between a mother and baby, a destructive container can be internalized – for example, a punitive superego-style containment that squashes any potential for experimental parts of the personality. Problems also result when the container is too rigid for what needs to be contained, or the contained is so explosive that the container is overwhelmed (Ferro, 1999).

Likewise, in analysis, the task of the analyst is to communicate to the patient the possibility of something new – an interaction between two people that can contain pain and result in mental growth. As the analysis progresses, this dynamic optimally will constantly evolve. The analyst, like the mother, needs to intuit her patient's feelings by "introjecting them, sustaining them, delaying action upon them so as to modify and modulate their impact . . . and thereby allow for their transformation or translation into useful meaning" (Grotstein, 1993: xiii). It is important to remember that for mother/infant and analyst/adolescent much cannot be said in articulate language, but instead must be intuited, to result in a thinking couple.

Bion's concept of container is sometimes equated with Winnicott's idea of holding. However, the concepts have different qualities (Ogden, 2004b). The holding environment is "positive and growth promoting" (Symington & Symington, 1996: 58). Containment can be either positive or negative, although the term is more often used in the positive meaning. Both the container and the contained are active in either integrative or destructive ways.

Next, I will discuss the K link, which Bion (1962: 90) sees as "essentially a function of two objects but it can be considered as a function of one," with the "earliest and most primitive manifestation of K occur[ring] in the relationship between mother and infant."

## The K link

Believing that "an emotional experience cannot be conceived of in isolation from a relationship" (Bion, 1962: 42), Bion designates three factors – L (Love), H (Hate) and K (Knowledge) – to stand for the predominant link the patient establishes in the hour with the therapist. He sees any human as endlessly involved in establishing a link with another, but the linking might be most exquisitely loving or ragefully destructive. The 'Knowledge' that Bion refers to as K is not static, but more verb than noun, involving the effort to get to know, to be receptive to, what is true of an experience. Bion focused on the K link in psychoanalysis as it "is the link that is germane to learning by experience" (1962: 47).

Bion's purpose in designating an L, H or K link is, in thinking about an hour retrospectively, to get at what was most true of the emotional experience of the hour. The effort to grapple with the nature of the link could give a key to the communication:

> [T]o sum up an emotional episode as K is to produce an imperfect record but a good starting point for the analyst's speculative meditation. In this regard the system I have sketched out, despite its crudity and naivety, possesses the rudiments of the essentials of a system of notation – record of fact and working tool.
>
> (1962: 44)

If an adolescent's desire to be known or to attack the possibility of being known seems predominant in an hour, then the K link would be the key to understanding his or her communication: "[T]he difference between the aim of the lie and the aim of truth can thus be expressed as a change of sense in x K y and to relate to intolerance of the pain associated with feelings of frustration" (Bion, 1962: 49).

If K appears predominant in a child's or adolescent's communication, then the type of K can be considered. Is the child trying to know herself or the object, or is the child too anxious to think about what goes on inside herself or another? If the child seems to be misunderstanding or denuding her experience, then the link is minus K. If the child is expressing in his play a sense that he has no hope of a capacity to think, then the key to the hour is 'no K.' O'Shaughnessy (1988: 182) describes 'no K' as when the child is "expressing in his material a psychotic condition in which he exists without the capacity to think." Although Bion suggests that one mode of linking L, H or K, would predominate in a session, he means this in the service of thinking rather than in a formulaic manner. Bion followed Klein in seeing envy as the primary motivation for attacking the ability to think (-K), but other motivations to misunderstand can also be considered.

Here is a brief example of an hour that can be thought about in terms of the K link. Elizabeth was a brilliant 7-year-old girl who attended a school for gifted children. Her parents, particularly her mother, were highly successful academics who divorced when Elizabeth was 3.

Her father, in particular, avoided emotions, which he chalked up to his British background. He was sent away to boarding school at 8. Elizabeth had started therapy six months earlier at the persistent urging of her school because of her emotional, relational and behavioral problems. Although gifted, Elizabeth's emotional understanding lags far behind her intellectual capacities.

Elizabeth settled quickly into therapy after what seemed to me to be an initial alertness to whether I would reject her. Soon after, the school reported behavioral, social and emotional improvement. During the school year, her mother had brought Elizabeth regularly to her weekly therapy sessions. When summer came, father did not bring Elizabeth to therapy during the two weeks he had her. Although there was an agreement to re-evaluate the therapy at six months, her father began raising concern that therapy would go on 'ad infinitum.' His opposition to and withdrawal from therapy was concerning. Additionally, my two-week vacation also interfered with meetings. In total, we missed five weeks of sessions over the summer.

In the session after this gap, Elizabeth came in and wanted to play the board game *Sorry*, which she played in a highly competitive manner, conveying that winning was everything. I felt aware of Elizabeth's intelligence and sensed a no-win situation; I would be a denigrated loser if I lost and Elizabeth would be left with a feeling she wasn't ready for if she lost. Feeling uneasy about my own competitive feelings, I commented on the competitive feeling and asked Elizabeth if she knew who was most competitive. Elizabeth said that she was. Then I asked who was more competitive, Elizabeth's mum or her dad? She replied, "My dad." I eventually won the game and Elizabeth immediately claimed she had won and picked up the playing pieces, ready to throw them in my face.

To return to our concepts: these communications could be thought of as attacks on K. Elizabeth's knowledge of losing the game was attacked, as was I, as the winner of the game. But in a larger sense there was an attack on any knowledge of loss or weakness. Elizabeth's environment was not supporting her need for continuity and this deprivation engendered a minus K link in her. Unable to think at an emotional level, father and daughter could only think well on a purely intellectual basis. In this hour, Elizabeth was unable to compete and maintain an emotional connectedness simultaneously. Here, the -K was an effort not to know how full of rage she was at her parents and her analyst for not sustaining the opportunity for emotional connection. For Elizabeth to be able to have a K link, it would also have meant having to know things that were acutely painful. The break in the consistency of the therapy was but one of many links that had been broken in her life. Father did not want mother to have contact with Elizabeth when Elizabeth was with him, nor did he want to have contact with Elizabeth when she was with her mother. It is overwhelming for a child to know when a parent cannot be containing, and instead is breaking links out of anger. This had been a disruptive external feature of Elizabeth's childhood, so it was not surprising that links got broken inside of her.

To generate a K link to her feelings about missing sessions would have brought Elizabeth close to Knowledge of her father's emotional absence from her and of her parents' emotional absence from each other. A link to K could bring relief at understanding but also pain at having to know.

A flight into action (being ready to throw the game pieces in the analyst's face) is not unusual in a young child whose internal resources are overwhelmed in relation to failures of containment. Bion describes -K in "the patient who appears to be unable to abstract, the patient to whom words are things – the things which the word is supposed to represent, but which are for him indistinguishable from their name and vice versa" (1962: 68–69). While a flight into action is far less out of step developmentally for a young child than for an adult, one could still describe this episode as -K. Bion saw all people as having psychotic aspects of the personality. While this child is only temporarily in a -K state, in this moment she was "destroying rather than promoting knowledge" (1962: 98) as the envy and pain related to her losses was too much to tolerate.

Schneider, in an elaboration of Bion's concept of -K, comments on the "survival value of not knowing" (2005: 837). Schneider sees Bion as largely discussing -K in terms of envy, but aware that -K "goes far beyond envy as its only, or even its primary, motivating force" (2005: 826). Schneider expands:

> We all are destined to psychically kill our parents in the act of growing up (Loewald, 1979) and to harbor incestuous wishes. Fortunately, we are usually able not to know about such horrifying truths until we are sufficiently mature (as children or adults) and helped by our parents

(or perhaps an analyst) to live with and make our peace with these human truths (along with other almost unbearable truths, such as the inescapability of our own death). Not knowing is, indeed, almost more important than knowing.

(2005: 828)

## Transformation of 'beta' into 'alpha'

Bion coined the terms 'alpha-elements' and 'beta-elements' to designate fundamental mental experiences. He conceives of humans as endlessly transforming beta-elements (raw sensory data and unprocessed emotions) into alpha-elements (units of meaningful experience which can be thought, linked and remembered), which he terms 'alpha function.' For Bion, dreaming is paradigmatic of alpha function and goes on, not just in sleep, but all of the time. Bion sees the fundamental purpose of analysis as the patient's gain in alpha function through the analyst's maternal reverie and the pair's shared dreaming, which leads to growth of the mind.

This view of dreaming sheds a particular light on play therapy. Ferro (1999) describes how various narrative derivatives are developed in child analysis through stories, play, drawing, dreaming, etc. Bion would see the play in play therapy as exactly right for the development of alpha function. Understanding of oneself is not generated in a linear manner, but instead through the grasp of central narratives that are never static but constantly developing. This process is going on in child, adolescent and adult analysis. However, the playfulness of play therapy has a lot to lend to our treatment of adolescents and adults. Bion states: "[D]ream-like memory is the memory [memories that float into the mind unbidden] of psychic reality and is the stuff of analysis . . . the dream and the psycho-analyst's working material both share dream-like quality" (1970: 70–71).

The play in play therapy allows the child a dream-like expression of her inner world, and allows the analyst a participation in the meanings of the child's inner world that become shared meanings. In play therapy, we become interpreters of dreams in the form of play. Unmetabolized raw emotions, such as Elizabeth's competitiveness and angry desire to throw the playing pieces in my face, are dreams in the hour.

The analyst interprets dreams in the form of comments on and participation in the play. We will now consider these ideas in relation to an adolescent in psychotherapy.

## 'Evie': transformations of beta into alpha

'Evie' began twice-weekly psychotherapy at 16. I was struck that she had the beauty of Botticelli's Venus, but dressed to look tough, sporting army boots. Prior neuropsychological testing had rendered diagnoses of ADHD, anxiety and depression. As a result, an earlier therapy had been attempted, which Evie did not settle into. Evie and her parents had broached the subject of therapy again after Evie had gotten very drunk. She had been taken to the emergency room and had her stomach pumped (following a fight with her best friend). Evie was also ambivalently taking anti-depressant medication. Evie's parents are prominent in their fields and make substantive contributions. In the initial telephone call Evie's mother described her daughter as the "anxious child of two tightly wound parents." Evie's mother saw Evie as feeling she could never meet her father's expectations.

When Evie first entered my office, she commented: "It smells nice in here." She told me that she felt "tired, sad and irritable. My mother doesn't know what is on my mind and school is hard." As the hour proceeded Evie went on to say: "My father is gross, the way he eats and the movements he makes with his mouth." She then told me about the fight with her best friend that led to her getting drunk. "I don't like my best friend's boyfriend; he's gross. I don't know what she's doing with him. The day I got drunk I was upset because she was making out with him." Despite Evie's prior reluctance to start therapy, I had the sense that the time was ripe now. She seemed to have frightened herself by losing consciousness when she was drunk. At the end of our first meeting Evie said: "I don't know how anything can change." I replied: "And yet you're here."

In a subsequent session Evie told me: "My parents put up with me. I'm a lot of trouble for them and I feel like a disappointment to them." As she spoke, my reverie was to similar feelings some adopted children express. I decided to tell Evie that her feelings reminded me of how some adopted children feel. To my surprise, Evie told me that she is adopted. While I had only met with Evie's parents once at this point (due to Evie's concern about her privacy), I was surprised that they had not told me such a significant fact.

Evie then told me that before she was born her mother had had a late miscarriage and that it was deemed unsafe for her to have another pregnancy. After telling me of her adoption Evie told me a dream. "I pierced my own lip. Everyone was, like, 'cool,' but I could see it was crooked and that was all I could think of." I thought that Evie was struggling with feeling that her difficulties (including feelings about her adoption and ADHD) were being glossed over. While the glossing-over likely came from protectiveness on her parents' part, Evie was left feeling difficulties could not be named. My reverie about adopted children seemed to lead to Evie's ability to begin to dream her emotional experience.

Evie's parents told me at our next meeting that they had not thought to mention Evie's adoption because they so experience her as their own child. I found their feeling touching, but thought that they had not considered what Evie's experience and fantasies of her adoption could be, particularly at this time of adolescent identity reorganization. Her parents' avoidance of emotions related to the adoption seemed to result in Evie feeling unable to reflect on important experiences inside her. The parents' avoidance prevented the growth of emotional Knowledge and provided too little containment for Evie. Evie's dream about her crooked piercing not being noticed could be understood as her being left to feel her own 'crookedness' could not be faced, just as her parents' sad struggle with miscarriage, infertility and the adoption were placed far away. Evie began to express curiosity about what her birth parents might be like and often wondered if someone who resembled her might be related to her.

Shortly after the above developments, Evie related a dream. "In the dream I was yelling at people and they don't stick around. But then I was able to write music and people were interested." Evie was embarrassed that the dream conveyed how irritable she could be. But the dream also seemed to depict a beginning experience of being able to make meaning and connect with others/me.

At this point Evie decided to reveal to her parents some of the abuse of alcohol that she had been revealing to me but hiding from them. Her parents were understandably worried and wanted to talk with me. I told them I understood their concern, but that I thought the most important element was that Evie was choosing to communicate to them about worrisome parts of herself (a movement out of -K into K).

I thought that Evie had been courageous to tell her parents about her excessive drinking. Evie's drinking seemed to occur when she felt overwhelmed. She was beginning to use the therapy to express her feelings instead of drowning them.

Despite this seeming progress, I received another call from Evie's mother that Evie had had a party at their home without permission while they were out. Father came home and found kids drunk and high. He also found LSD and mushrooms. Evie was very upset when she was caught and made vague references to hurting herself. Weeping, she told her parents: "You don't know what I'm going through, you don't know anything about me. I'm not happy with my life. I don't want to go to college. I'm not a good person. Why do you love me?" Her parents told Evie they loved her and that that wouldn't change but that they also wanted to meet with me to try to understand what was going on with her.

Evie did not like the idea of her parents talking with me about this interlude without being there. However, she also felt panicked at the idea of being present for the meeting. I suggested that she might want me to help her to articulate her experience to her parents. I thought that she felt inarticulate with her highly articulate parents. I told Evie that I thought she would need to find a way to be more comfortable and competent in discussing things, including her alcohol and drug use.

There are many considerations in breaking the frame of an individual therapy to have a joint meeting with parents. I take this step at times of crisis. In this case I felt that the parents' concerns were reasonable and that Evie needed help in communicating with them. I also felt that the parents would feel too sent away at this point to refer them to a colleague.

In the family meeting Evie faced away from her parents, but gave me permission to speak for her. I told her parents: "While you mean well in communicating with Evie, she processes things at a different speed and you need to hang in there with her." I told them: "Evie feels insecure in relation to what she imagines would have been a better child if mother been able to carry her pregnancy to term." Evie's parents expressed some anger that they felt Evie did not listen to them, but also were able to hear that Evie frequently felt they also didn't tell her things. (Evie frequently expressed that her parents were behind closed doors "conferencing" about her.) I advocated that they continue to try to talk as a family, awkward as it might be. In this case I thought that the growth of the parents as containers could also facilitate Evie's development of internal containment. After this meet-ing Evie's parents were willing to start a piece of psychoanalytic parent work with a colleague. When parents are willing (along with their adoles-cent) to face emotional Knowledge, adolescents can feel accompanied and less alone in the hard work of growing up.

As is so often the case in the treatment of adolescents, academic tim-ing began to intrude. At this point Evie was a senior in high school. Evie went off her medications in the midst of the anxiety of the college testing and application process without discussing this decision with her parents or me. Evie expressed discomfort with "depending" on medications. She was also uncomfortable with the help she needed from her mother and from me. I acknowledged with Evie that the help from her mother, myself and her medication felt like a blow to her autonomy. Evie played a song for me that she felt captured her feelings at this col-lege application juncture. The songwriter expresses that he was raised to feel unique, but that this was misguided. He now would rather just be part of some machine serving a purpose. But even that he doesn't know how to accomplish.

These lyrics reflected Evie's feeling that her parents had not helped her to have a realistic view of her problems. They had always treated her as special, but now she was faced with impersonal aspects of the college admissions process. She felt her parents fobbed her off onto me to deal with her problems. I told her that she had also not been direct with me about going off her medications. I said it was not a good pattern to develop to avoid dealing with me directly instead of dealing with me (or others) face to face.

Evie was struggling with how to integrate what meaning having a neuro-developmental disorder (ADHD) had for her. I empathized with her wish that it was not so, and with her confusion about how to think about it.

Evie was accepted to good colleges and chose a school connected to real intellectual passions. As we faced termination Evie wanted to cut back to once a week. I told her I thought that would avoid painful feelings about our ending. As she had communicated with me so often through music, I told her the lyrics of a song that called another to come out and come here. I said I thought she should be here for the ending with her whole self. Evie agreed not to cut back and brought me a poem about mourning. In her last session Evie gave me a pin-cushion as a going-away present to acknowledge how prickly she had often been during our work. Her gift seemed to capture her mixture of affection and irritability. While we only had two years together and unresolved problems were left for a later date, I felt that we had been 'in something' as Bion advises, instead of merely talking about something. Work with many adolescents creates a special heat and press to be 'in something.'

Some child analysts feel work with adolescents is quite partial when they 'resist' finding their own words for their feelings. Evie did often communicate through song lyrics, poems, drawings and even the final pincushion. Further development for Evie might be in an increasing ability to name her own feelings. However, I think Evie found the ways that suited her to communicate with me. She had likewise claimed numerous forms of translating beta into alpha – music, writing, literature, drawing, and dreaming.

## Conclusion

Bion's inter-related concepts, such as container/contained, maternal reverie and the development of thinking through alpha function, are highly applicable to the treatment of adolescents and children. His conceptualizations of thinking and non-thinking states (K or -K links) underlie the possibility for development in children and adolescents, that is, of 'learning from experience'. I have tried to show how -K states in parents are experienced by their children. In the next chapter I will turn to a Bionian conceptualization of the intensities of work with parents of adolescents.

## Acknowledgment

This chapter is partly based on: Brady, M., Tyminski, R., & Carey, K. (2012). To know or not to know: An application of Bion's K and -K to child treatment. *Journal of Child Psychotherapy, 38*(3): 302–317.

## Notes

1  As is well known, Klein was Bion's second analyst. Klein cited her analysis of young children as the most fundamental source of her thinking.
2  Bion uses *mother* to refer to the infant's primary object; it could equally be a father.

# References

Bion, W.R. (1962). *Learning from Experience*. London: Karnac.

Bion, W.R. (1970). Attention and interpretation. In *Seven Servants*. New York, NY: Jason Aronson.

Bion, W.R. (2005). *The Tavistock Seminars*. London: Karnac.

Brown, L.J. (2012). Bion's discovery of Alpha Function: Thinking under fire on the battlefield and in the consulting room. *International Journal of Psychoanalysis, 93*: 1191–1214.

Ferro, A. (1999). *The Bi-Personal Field: Explorations in Child Analysis*. London: Routledge.

Grotstein, J. (1993). In Bion, W.R. *Second Thoughts: Selected Papers on Psychoanalysis*. New York: Jason Aronson, ix–xiv.

Klein, M. (1975). Notes on some schizoid mechanisms. In *Envy and Gratitude*. London: The Hogarth Press, pp. 1–24 (First published in 1946.)

Loewald, H. (1979). The waning of the Oedipus complex. *Journal of the American Psychoanalytic Association, 27*: 751–776.

O'Shaughnessy, E. (1988). W.R. Bion's theory of thinking and new techniques in child analysis. In E. Bott-Spillius (Ed.), *Melanie Klein Today: Developments in Theory and Practice, Volume I: Mainly Theory*. London: Routledge.

Ogden, T.H. (2004a). An introduction to the reading of Bion. *International Journal of Psychoanalysis, 85*: 285–300.

Ogden, T.H. (2004b). On holding and containing, being and dreaming. *International Journal of Psychoanalysis, 85*: 1349–1364.

Schneider, J.A. (2005). Experiences in K and K. *International Journal of Psychoanalysis, 86*: 825–839.

Symington, J., & Symington, N. (1996). *The Clinical Thinking of Wilfred Bion*. New York: Routledge.

# Chapter 7

# Parent work in adolescent analysis

## An application of Bion's group theory

'Noel,' a 14-year-old girl in analysis, knows that I have a son, as she had a chance encounter on the street with us. While adamant that she needs no parental intervention with her binge drinking, she imagines that I would be stricter with my own son than I am with her. Clearly, she rightly envisions parental authority as an aspect of love. This brief vignette captures something of why parent work in adolescent analysis is a 'hot topic.' Analysts walk a difficult path of protecting adolescents' privacy to some degree. We must bear knowing about some things parents would rightly be concerned about without revealing them. Conversely, we must keep in mind the need for parental authority. When parents are able to establish conditions of safety for their adolescents, analysts are on much easier ground. However, it is a too-frequent scenario that parents let go of reasonable supervision of their adolescents, sometimes in response to normal adolescent developmental shifts, withdrawals and provocations. Weariness is commonplace in parents of adolescents. Work with parents of younger children can be challenging, but analysts working with parents of adolescents face additional problems.

Parental unavailability often underlies risk-taking in adolescence. Risk-taking can escalate in an effort to engage parents' attention. Collateral work with parents of adolescents is aimed at helping them to understand these communications. However, in some families there are real limitations to parents' willingness or ability to carry the challenges of parenting an adolescent. An inherent tension surfaces in the treatment of adolescents between remaining an analyst and assuming parental functions. I might feel worried that my work and relationship with an adolescent will not be enough to prevent some tragedy, just as any parent's worst nightmare is that some combination of bad judgment and chance could take their child from them. I think there is something irreducible about filling some parental roles with some adolescents while analyzing the effects of doing so. In this chapter I will discuss parent work in adolescent analysis with the help of Bion's group theory.

## Parent work informed by Bion's group theory

Adolescent treatment confronts the analyst with the individual and the family group simultaneously. In work with parents of adolescents in psychotherapy or psychoanalysis, Bion's insights about group functioning help us conceptualize the unconscious group processes and relations active within the family, which interact with the unconscious intrapsychic processes and object relations active within the adolescent.

*Parent work* (or *collateral parent work*) is work with parents focused on understanding their adolescent and their parenting, in conjunction with the psychoanalysis or psychotherapy of their child,[1] as distinct from family therapy, in which the family is regularly seen together (Graham, 1998). After an initial evaluation of the adolescent and an agreement for treatment, the analyst usually sees the parents for ongoing meetings, separate from the teen's sessions, throughout the treatment.[2] Parent meetings are kept separate from the teen's individual sessions in order to allow a private space for the teen's internal and external concerns to unfold.[3] The frequency of meetings with parents is controversial. Minimal parent meetings allow the adolescent to bring his or her internal world to the treatment with the least interference and maximum privacy. On the other hand, a meaningful adolescent treatment can be interrupted because of an insufficient alliance with the parents. The autonomy of the adolescent work needs to be balanced with enough contact with the parents to foster their commitment to it, as well as potentially helping the adolescent by intervening with the parents. My own practice is to schedule joint meetings with the parents and adolescent only in emergencies. Parent work may include interpretations of unconscious difficulties in parental or familial functioning, if the parent(s) agrees to examine such issues. Parent work also includes developmental issues in the adolescent, as well as parent guidance.

Adolescent analysis can model itself too narrowly on adult analysis and underemphasize the extent to which the adolescent is embedded within the family. Bion (2005a: 18; original presentation, 1977) comments that in analysis it is misleading to think there is apparently only one person there with the analyst: "[A] group is almost like one person, character or personality, spread over a space . . . in the group one could then locate, so to speak, the origin, the source, of the infection." Although child analysts have long recognized the importance of the parents and other aspects of the environment as contributors to the child's psychopathology, the trouble has been in formulating a coherent set of concepts to apply to parent work.

Bion highlights the fundamental tension between the individual in any group and the child in any family: "The individual is a group animal at war, not simply with the group, but with himself for being a group animal and with those aspects of his personality that constitute his 'groupishness'" (1961: 168). I will discuss three areas in which I think Bion's ideas can usefully illuminate the role of the family in child or adolescent analysis: clinical attitudes toward work with parents, *work group* and *basic assumption group* functioning within the family, and the *group culture* represented through behaviors in the family arising from tensions between individual psychology and group mentality. First, I will briefly review the literature pertinent to work with parents or families influenced by Bion's group theory.

## Review of the Literature

Despite the notable and increasing presence of Bion's ideas in many child and adolescent analysts' writings (Alvarez, 1992; Anderson, 1998; Ferro, 2006; O'Shaughnessy, 1964; Waddell, 1998; Williams, 1998), I was unable to locate any literature regarding work with parents of adolescents or children derived from Bionian group theory. This may be due in part to the tendency in the UK (where Bion's ideas have affected child treatment more than they have in the United States) to have one therapist or analyst treat the child and another therapist work with the parents or family. In the United States, the practice is more often, though not always, that the child analyst or therapist also works with the parents collaterally. However, Bionian conceptualizations of group functioning are well represented in two separate modes of family treatment, one developed at the Tavistock Clinic in London, the other developed by object relations family therapists in the United States.

### The Tavistock approach

Graham describes a particular way of thinking about family work, which evolved in the Adolescent Department of the Tavistock Clinic.

He notes: "Given the ordinariness or ubiquity of the family unit within society it is somewhat surprising that those influenced by psychoanalytic theory have studied the family considerably less than they have studied individuals, or groups of unrelated individuals" (1998: 143).

Citing Bion as the psychoanalyst who has provided us with the most useful understanding of group dynamics, Graham advocates describing for a family the inherent tensions (elucidated by Bion) between "desires for individual expression and a longing for total immersion within the activities of the group" (1998: 146). Either element might be taken up interpretively in family work – the anxieties related to individual development or to family group identity.

Graham underlines the importance of a family identity. "Sometimes a family comes for help, almost with a sense of despair that they are a family in name only, wanting someone to tell them they are a family" (1998: 146). He describes the simultaneous levels of individual and group dynamics that are so interesting in the treatment of children:

> Just as Melanie Klein showed how each individual has a number of internal figures, internal objects, in their mind, the relationship to whom provides a lens through which the world is seen, so there is a similar process within families. At quite unspoken, unconscious levels there appear to be joint phantasies, or shared internal figures, which may represent shared beliefs about the nature of certain relationships.
>
> (1998: 154)

## Object relations family therapy

Bion's group relations theory has also strongly affected object relations family therapy.

Roger Shapiro, an analyst and family therapist, was one of the first to become aware of the relevance of Bionian conceptions of small group dynamics and projective identification to work with families, and participated in two Bionian group relations working conferences (Scharff, 1989: 7). Scharff describes how Shapiro's personal experience of projective identification (his own and others') in group interaction cut through his previous ego psychology background and led to his developing an appreciation for Kleinian and Bionian theory.[4]

In their observations of families, Shapiro and Zinner describe "coordinated, shared, complementary behavior in the family related to a level of unconscious fantasy and defense in the family analogous to Bion's (1961) concept of small group behavior organization and particular unconscious assumptions" (1971: 82). Shapiro and Zinner use Bion's conceptions of primitive and advanced functioning in groups to understand progressive and regressive movements in families. Bion describes these two levels of functioning, which he considers active in all groups, as *work group functioning* and *basic assumption group functioning.* I will describe these two concepts in detail below.[5]

Scharff notes that, in family therapy, "we analyze the family's resistance to being helped and our own resistances against involving ourselves in painful family experience" (1989: 11). She continues:

> [L]ike Bion's groups, families are small groups doing their work of facing a series of developmental challenges that raise anxiety. This anxiety is defended against by mutual projective identification processes that give rise to various subgroup formations . . . One common defense is that of delineation of an individual as sick . . . this occurs by projection of bad, unwanted parts of the self into one unconsciously designated recipient in order to keep the family good.
>
> (1989: 20–21)

This situation is common in the beginning of an individual psychotherapy with an adolescent as well. Although the teenager may need individual treatment in her own right (perhaps in part to begin to understand how such projections have influenced her internal world), therapists should be aware of the likelihood that anxieties in the family will intensify when the adolescent no longer serves as the recipient of pathogenic projections.

Zinner and Shapiro's thinking assimilates Bion's insights regarding the communicative use of projective identification and the splitting off of valued as well as unwanted parts of the internal object world:

> [T]he parent's projection of elements of his own previously internalized relations serve not only a defensive function but also a restorative one to bring back to life in the form of the offspring the parent's own lost objects, both good and bad.
>
> (1972: 526)

Zinner and Shapiro also examine the (mainly unconscious) readiness of an adolescent to receive a projection: "[T]he motivation which may need to be most reckoned with is the adolescent's fear of object loss which might ensue were he not to act on behalf of the parent's defensive organization" (1972: 526). As analysts, we struggle to differentiate when an adolescent has an intrapsychic anxiety related to his or her own growth (perhaps based on fantasies of his or her own developing sexuality or aggression) and when growth *is* actually dangerous within a family group.

Shapiro (1989) writes that the intimacy and history of a family life make for differences from the "stranger groups" that Bion and his group therapy successors (Ganzarain, 1989; Kreeger, 1975; Lawrence, Bain & Gould, 1996) treated. Nonetheless, he maintains how important it is to the treatment of families to observe shifts between reality tasks (i.e., work group functioning) to family behavior dominated by unconscious assumptions (i.e., basic assumption group functioning).

## Clinical Attitudes toward Work with Parents

First, I will examine a potential clinical attitude underlying work with parents of adolescents in analysis or psychotherapy. This work can be greeted as out of the stream of our best functioning as analysts. It can be thought of as information gathering or as maintaining a connection with parents. But analysts seldom seem to engage in it with the same subtlety and complexity as we bring to our work with individual patients. Actually, a session with parents is no less an analytic hour than any other hour, yet here the interpretations are focused primarily on the functioning of the family. I am reminded of Bion's comment that the "only point of importance in any session is the unknown" (1967: 260). A moment of surprise or affective intensity may be the central focus of an hour with parents.

In a recent hour, I found myself struggling to make sense of an incident that the parents related to me. They reported an episode in which it was ambiguous whether their teenage daughter had been sexually assaulted by a boy. They were acquainted with the boy's parents, had considered having him arrested, but had never raised their concerns with his parents. I struggled internally to make sense of their handling of the situation and noted to them that I was puzzled that they had not raised their concerns with the boy's parents. At the time, I was just getting to know these parents and this oversight felt meaningful. They replied that they thought they had been too much influenced by their daughter's initial wish to put the incident to rest. Our discovering a potential meaning together allowed this issue to be noted in an emotionally alive way for our ongoing consideration. We jointly discovered a tendency to falter in their parental role for their teenage daughter, due to their fear of conflict with her.

Such an approach would not be unusual for any clinician employing his or her countertransference in work with parents, but I wish to emphasize the focus on countertransference, which is the underpinning of the Bionian concepts to be discussed below. Bion writes that the root of an idea for an interpretation "is in the relationship . . . There is something that rapidly comes to exist when there are two people in the room . . . So the germ of an idea really belongs to both" (2005b: 21). The most important interpretations made to parents come from the analyst's emotional experience with them. Bion writes:

> I sometimes think that an analyst's feelings while taking a group – feelings while absorbing the basic assumptions of the group – are one of the few bits of what scientists might call evidence, because he can know what he is feeling. I attach great importance to feelings for that reason.
>
> (2005b: 105)

This perspective goes along with my view of the analyst of an adolescent as the recipient of a stream of projective identifications related to different issues within the family. Through the interpersonal interaction with the family, a pressure is exerted on the analyst to think, feel and act in ways congruent with the unconscious fantasies shared within the family (Ogden, 1982: 12).

Sometimes I will interpret a specific connection between a parent's psychology and that of the adolescent. These interpretations are important, and seem to be the sort of interpretations child analysts are well trained to make (Fraiberg, Adelson & Shapiro, 1975). I think we are less prepared, however, to make interpretations that address the intricate functioning of the larger family group. In discussing his work with groups, Bion remarks:

> I used to be beguiled into giving individual interpretations as in psychoanalysis. In doing this I was doing what patients often do – trying to get to individual treatment. True, I was trying to get to it as a doctor,

but in fact this can be stated in terms of an attempt to get rid of the "badness" of the group and, for the doctor, the "badness" of the group is its apparent unsuitability as a therapeutic instrument . . . instead [one can] regard this unsuitability as a function of the failure of the doctor or patient to use the group in a therapeutic way.

(1961: 115–116)

Bion views the analyst's urge to make individual interpretations within a group as his or her being drawn into an authoritative role, evoked by the group's dependency wishes. Instead, he suggests that an analyst's comments should focus on the way the group is functioning, including how it uses the analyst. Although the analyst is not literally a member of the family, she or he is ineluctably drawn into its group dynamics. By seeing myself as a part of a new group that is now established, I hope to see how I am being affected by the functioning of the entire group.

For example, I found that I had accepted the acrimonious unwillingness of one set of divorced parents to meet together on behalf of their 15-year-old daughter, 'Leslie.' I am not making a point about the potential benefit or necessity of separate meetings in working with some divorced parents. But I too-easily accepted the parents' unwillingness to put Leslie's needs before their own bitterness and had unconsciously adopted an aspect of this group's functioning. I began to insist on some meetings with both parents together to attempt to establish work group functioning. In fact, the parents' lack of co-parental responsibility had contributed to an escalation in Leslie's symptoms. She brought a life-threatening issue to my attention, and it required my telling her that we needed to meet together with her parents. I felt that all the anxiety about Leslie had been deposited in me by her and her parents. I urged her to tell her parents of her risk-taking, which she agreed to. We agreed to a conjoint session with her, her parents and myself in order for her to tell them of the risks she was taking. The most breathtaking moment in my work with these parents occurred in this meeting when Leslie told her parents that she and her siblings "could drive a truck through" their lack of parental coordination. I then directly challenged the parents' unwillingness to work together, and, though the work remained difficult, some improvement in parental cooperation occurred. My unconscious collusion with the parents' pervasive avoidance of responsibility helped me to identify the way this lack of responsibility for Leslie's safety was being internalized within Leslie's character.

## Work Group and Basic Assumption Functioning in the Family

Bion depicts a constant tension in groups between progressive and regressive forces. This dialectic is equally true within family groups where inevitable tensions promote or impede individual development. For example, Bion describes the possibility of individual distinctiveness leading a group to a state of panic (1961: 142), which is a common problem in the interaction of individual and family functioning when a child reaches adolescence. Bion believes that the minimum size of a group is three. "Two members have personal relationships; with three or more there is a change of quality (interpersonal relationship)" (1961: 26). Any family has at a minimum two parents and a child, even if one parent is only present as an internal representation.

Bion views every group as consisting of work group functioning and basic assumption functioning. Growing maturity in a group could be reflected in a greater awareness of the basic assumption tendencies of the group. Bion identified three primary basic assumption modes in groups – the dependency group, the pairing group, and the fight–flight group – and saw these modes as potentially shifting, but always with one mode of basic assumption in ascendance at any particular time.

### Work group functioning

Bion (1961) defines 'work group' processes as the group's capacity for rational cooperation to 'do' something. He wrote:

> I attribute great force and influence to the work group, which through its concern with reality is compelled to employ the methods of science in no matter how rudimentary a form. I think one of the striking things about a group is that despite the influence of the basic assumptions, it is the W group that triumphs in the long run.
>
> (1961: 135)

Work group processes in a family could involve the effort to balance the needs and desires of all the members. For example, deciding to bring a child to treatment could indicate work group functioning in a family – the effort to grapple realistically with a problem in the child or family. Parental love for children provides strong impetus to work group tendencies and the motivation to face significant problems in a family. "Basic assumption" aspects of groups, however, constantly perturb work group goals.

### Basic assumption functioning

Bion described the ineluctable tendency for groups to descend into basic assumption modes:

> [P]articipation in basic assumption activity requires no training, experience, or mental development. It is instantaneous, inevitable and instinctive . . . In contrast with work group function basic assumption activity makes no demands on the individual for a capacity to cooperate but depends on the individual's possession of what I call valency – a term I borrow from the physicists to express a capacity for instantaneous involuntary combination of one individual with another for sharing and acting on a basic assumption.
>
> (1961: 135)

### Dependency

A group functioning under the basic assumption of dependency is motivated by the wish to be sustained by a leader on whom it depends for nourishment, material and emotional, as well as protection. One example of this is the tendency in some families to give free rein to a father who is not expected to develop or grow as others in the families are because he needs to be seen as invulnerable. To allow him to have struggles and problems would be to challenge the basic assumption of dependency. In such families, the father's strength may be rather hollow because he is never really expected to grapple with any internal difficulty, as the mother and children need to excessively idealize him in order to avoid anxious uncertainty.

The father of 'Catherine,' a 16-year-old girl with a history of cutting, stopped attending our parent meetings without any comment or discussion. The sense was that emotions were not his area and that he was leaving these issues to his wife.[6] His forte was his business success and role as a spectacular breadwinner for the family. My countertransference experience was of myself, and, more important, Catherine, being unseen by her father. I thought this experience of invisibility was contributing to Catherine's need to make her problems visible through cutting.

In an individual session, Catherine told me that her father had yelled at her and been physically rough with her. She felt frightened of his anger. Her mother was present and, though she did not like the father's roughness, said nothing. I felt that this sort of incident was in milder form a recapitulation of mother's family dynamics – which were disturbingly dominated by a man in authority who got away with things and was not challenged. I thought that it was harmful for my patient to witness her mother not being able to take a stand with her father (her mother not being sufficiently independent) and to thus experience men as having an overwhelming force. I asked both parents to come in to talk about the incident. I told them I thought it was important for their daughter to see that her mother had talked to her father and made it clear that he had been too rough.

With Catherine I explored the meanings of male power in her family and the role for women of being admirable but with little control over anything but their own bodies. I had experienced this family's expectation that the father be held above dealing with me or with his daughter's problems. This exempting of father impeded his development and the family's development of a capacity to face problems together.

## Pairing

In a group where pairing operates as a basic assumption, unconscious motivation is aroused to support

> two members who will produce a new leader-figure who will assume full responsibility for the group's security. The unconscious phantasy reflects a wish that the pair will produce a Messiah, a Saviour, either in the form of a person or an organizing idea round which they can cohere.
>
> (Lawrence et al., 1996)

This issue is common in families because parents can come together with many unconscious hopes to produce a child, sometimes including the hope that the child can deliver them from a sense of failure and lack, making the child a repository of grand hope. Such a pervasive hope can become problematic when, for some reason, the child is not able to serve that role, e.g., when the child is burdened with a severe pathology. In that case, the child cannot stand for the utopian hopes of the parents but instead represents a terrible reminder of their own failures. Problems can also develop when pairing impedes individual or family development.

Pairing was the basic assumption operating in the family of 'Mario,' a 14-year-old boy I was treating for school phobia (discussed at length in Chapter 2). The parents acknowledged entrenched, long-standing marital difficulties, and Mario seemed drawn into a pair with his mother in order to deny the anxiety everyone in the family would otherwise feel about the absent pairing between the parents. Mario seemed to be his mother's son with little connection to his father.

In a phone call, the mother told me the father had an escalating gambling addiction. She was adamant that I not let her husband know that I was aware of this addiction. I felt little possibility in the phone conversation to help her consider this position. I felt drawn into a pairing with the mother by being given knowledge that I was not to let on to father. Not long afterwards, Mario and his mother had a terrible argument that started when Mario became angry that his mother had not left a pencil where it was usually kept, as he wanted to write me a note. The fight escalated to the point that Mario threatened suicide. Mother left me an accusatory phone message, implying the treatment was not helping the boy, yet was unwilling to talk with me directly. I felt anxious at the blaming nature of the interaction and the potential for acting out, or interruption of the treatment.

Because the mother was avoiding my calls, I sent a letter to the parents and said that it was urgent that we meet together to address the turmoil in the family. I thought that Mario unconsciously felt that his mother was not providing him a link to his father, as represented in the absent pencil. Further, that as the basic assumption in the family was around pairing, that the new pairing between the boy and me was perceived as a threat to the pairing of mother/son that was unconsciously intended to stave off acute anxiety at the disintegrating family.

When I met with the parents I said:

*A:*    I want to hear your thoughts about the terrible upset that has occurred.
*F:*    I wasn't there. My son called me – he didn't like it that his mother had called you.

Literally, the father was not present, but he was also not present by absenting himself in the gambling addiction and because of his fear of blame.

*A:*    It is important to notice that your son wanted to reach you for help with a difficulty with his mother.

When I asked the mother her thoughts she told me:

*M:*    The fight was a horror and I try not to think about it.
*A:*    I understand wanting to put it out of mind, but it is part of being a mother to find a way to talk about the rough spots in the family.
*M:*    I know you're right.
*A:*    I don't necessarily see the issue as just between you and Mario, but possibly as part of the larger problem in the family. Because of the problems in the marriage it seems hard for mother to serve as a bridge to father at a time when Mario is becoming a man.
*F:*    To whatever extent that's true, that she's not a bridge to me or I to her, I also think our son would have trouble with her anyway in the way I do. She is very controlling in insisting on togetherness and it's not easy to deal with.
*A:*    Mario is growing up; he needs to be close to his mother, but also to find his own way.

This parent session was just a step in dealing with complex familial problems, but I thought it went in the direction of naming certain issues in the family. Unconsciously, the family was operating with a basic assumption that the parental pair would be replaced by mother's pairing with the son, and a new salvation would be created to prevent anxiety. Mario was pulled in as his mother's confidante, just as I had been in the mother's phone call. This alliance with his mother, however, prevented Mario real psychological access to his father. I believe that the fight was Mario's unconscious effort to break out of the pairing with his mother, which was preventing his development. Naming these issues in the parent session allowed some return to work group functioning of appropriate parental roles and responsibilities to support their son's development and acknowledge some of the problems in the family.

### Fight–flight

In a fight–flight basic assumption group, the unconscious motivation occasions either fighting something or running away from it. Bion noted: "[P]anic flight and uncontrolled attack are really the same" (1961: 179).

One example of basic assumption motivation resulting in fight–flight that I observed in a family entailed the parents allowing their 10-year-old son to say outrageously destructive and violent things to them. I was shocked by the insults this boy would hurl at his parents. The child's powerful expression of aggression conveyed a rage operating in the family that had been pushed out of awareness. The family fled any effort to grapple with rage or hatred amongst them by allowing the son to be the identified raging patient.

Another example of primitive anxieties handled by fight–flight occurred in a family of a boy I treated in which the father had a life-threatening illness. The family was often caught in repetitive and acrimonious fighting. I, too, felt caught in an endless repetition. Though the fighting was painful, it largely served as a familiar distraction from the terrible anxieties evoked by the father's potential decline and death. I interpreted the fighting to both the parents and separately to their son as a familiar but painful way of coming together to flee the dread the family was facing. I emphasized that we would face these fears together. As I interpreted this horrific fear and defense, the family was more able to accept and share the terrors they felt with each other and with me.

## Development as a Threat

Bion (1961) describes the emergence of something new in a group as threatening, and demanding of development. Groups functioning under one of the basic assumptions are unable to tolerate development. This could be an apt description of the problem at hand when child treatment stirs something new in the child and, indirectly, in the family. Frequently, development can be met with a hostile response by the basic assumption mentality, whereas the work group understands the need to develop. The following incident brought these issues home to me.

I had treated 'Stavros,' now 11 years old, for six years in analysis. He had severe separation anxiety and concurrent uncontrolled aggression when he started treatment, to the point that his mother had to accompany him to kindergarten and stay with him there every day. Stavros' problems consumed an enormous amount of energy within the family. Several years later, when he was much improved, and the end of the analysis seemed in sight, his parents abruptly stopped paying for the treatment and refused to schedule any further sessions with me, although they continued to bring Stavros for his sessions. Dismayed by the parents' withdrawal, I was afraid that this long-standing analysis would end in a manner that could undermine Stavros' progress.

Phone calls with the mother revealed a negative maternal transference. She felt I did not really care about her difficulties. I realized that, although Stavros' progress had made it evident that real growth was possible, the parents still were saddled with (mostly) the same neurotic problems they had when Stavros began treatment. I engaged the mother when she came to collect Stavros and acknowledged her ongoing depression and feeling of burden. (Earlier, I had referred the mother for her own treatment, which she had not pursued.) I said that although we could all be proud of the progress Stavros had made, I also thought she had wanted me to notice that she and her husband had not felt sufficiently attended to. Although the work I was able to do with these parents in the termination phase was limited, the focus on the larger family issues allowed the parents to feel adequately understood in order to end their son's treatment with warm and cooperative feelings. The mother has kept in occasional contact with me over many years, so I know that some positive connection has been sustained.

This experience was a turning point for me. It indicated the depth of attention that needs to be paid to parents being threatened by development in their child while their child is in therapy or analysis. I had been lulled by the apparent progress of the individual work.

## Group Mentality and Group Culture in the Family

### Group mentality

Another important Bionian conceptualization that applies to families is 'group mentality.' Bion writes:

> Group mentality is the unanimous expression of the will of the group, contributed to by the individual in ways of which he is unaware, influencing him disagreeably whenever he thinks or behaves in a manner at variance with the basic assumptions.

> (1961: 65)

Families can exert subtle unconscious pressure on individuals in order to preserve the functioning of the group (i.e., family) even to the extreme of a willingness to sacrifice the individual. The parents of 'Anna' operated under a basic assumption of flight (i.e., evasion of all discomfort and, therefore, any acknowledgment of their daughter's problems). I felt that they were too willing to let their 16-year-old daughter have substance-abuse problems. Anna's addiction problems were another manifestation of flight in the family – flight to numb or high states – in order to preserve the status quo of evasion in the family. The only thing the parents seemed to agree upon was minimizing Anna's problems.

Anna and I had been struggling together for several months over her escalating substance abuse when she came in and told me she had passed out the previous evening after drinking and had vomited in her sleep. I knew that she was frightened to think about her addiction and about the changes that would be required for it to be treated. I told her that it was important for the whole truth to come out with her parents. We met with her parents, and despite making light of the problem, they did agree that Anna would enter an intensive outpatient substance-abuse treatment program while continuing her analysis. Despite Anna's anger at me, my insistence that this problem be faced signaled to her that I took her problems seriously. Although her parents' response was not ideal they did become more engaged than they had been. Together, we were able to shift from a basic assumption group functioning in the mode of flight to taking up the real work group functioning needed to adequately treat Anna's substance abuse. The group mentality shifted from one in which anxieties had to be denied at all costs to one in which some anxieties could be faced. Bion (1961) views group mentality as causing difficulties for the individual. With Anna, her need to have her disturbances recognized could be sacrificed to the group mentality of evasion of difficulties.

### Group culture

Bion coined the term *group culture* "to describe those aspects of the behavior of the group which seemed to be born of the conflict between group mentality and the desires of the individual" (1961: 59–60). Each family has a different tolerance (expressed consciously and unconsciously) regarding the needs of the individual in the family group. A common expression of this can be found in families that become unbalanced when an individual member begins to develop in an individual manner, thinking for himself or herself. At the other extreme, there are families who prize individuality or rebelliousness to the extent that they have difficulty imposing any structure or expectations on their children.

Another aspect of group culture is how leadership is displayed within the group. Bion said that he liked to probe the confusing and obscure functioning of a group "by considering what position in the emotions of the group I myself occupy at any given moment, and I like to observe . . . the sort of leadership that is being exercised by others in the group" (1961: 59).

When I began work with the parents of 'Joseph,' an eight-year-old phobic boy, I initially thought that I had led the parents in a productive direction, by linking Joseph's fears with the intense unresolved anger between them, which spilled over onto their son in numerous ways. I recommended a referral for couples therapy, and suggested that we would continue to address times when their marital problems affected their son. When I next met with the parents, however, the mother demanded a behavioral solution to Joseph's problems, without a sense that his problems had any link to the conflicts in the family or even with his own underlying emotional states. Although the father was somewhat more open to connecting these issues, mother avoided contact with me for some time, which father assented to. The mother was leading by a passive-aggressive avoidance of me, which was tacitly allowed by father, because he too was afraid of facing the complex marital problems.

As Bion notes: "[U]nless a group actively disavows a leader it is, in fact, following him" (1961: 58). This mother's active attempts to de-link the meanings of Joseph's problems led him (until significant work was done in the therapy) to feel that his fearfulness was just the way he was. This example also demonstrates the complex problem in the collateral work of parents' willingness (or lack thereof) to investigate their own contributions to their child's problems.

It is essential for clinicians to make explicit with parents whether they are willing to look at their contribution to troubles in the family. The parent work described in this article can be deeply meaningful and helpful when parents convey some openness to it, but, of course, it is circumscribed if conscious or unconscious unwillingness or fear is too great.

## Conclusion

Work with parents is often the most difficult and certainly the most under-conceptualized aspect of child analysis (Brady, 2006; Novick & Novick, 2005). However, when the analyst can address family issues in depth, building on the intrapsychic work with the child or adolescent, the result can be a unique synergy in which changes in the adolescent can contribute to changes in the family and vice versa. For a change in a child or adolescent through psychotherapy to be sustained, it is likely that the family as a group will need to develop, just as the individual child will need to develop. Bion saw groups as both hopelessly committed to, as well as hateful toward, the process of development.

I hope this chapter will contribute to the difficult work of conceptualizing unconscious family group dynamics in analytic adolescent treatment. Although Bion saw the potential for psychotic anxieties as always present in a group, he also believed that "intellectual activity of a high order is possible in a group together with an awareness (and not an evasion) of the emotions of the basic assumption groups" (1961: 175). Parents' experiences of an analytic understanding of their family functioning, although often challenging, also gives them the clearest opportunity to perceive the nature of the analytic work one is struggling to accomplish with their child.

## Acknowledgment

This chapter is based upon: Brady, M.T. (2011). The individual in the group: An application of Bion's group theory to parent work in child analysis and child psychotherapy. *Contemporary Psychoanalysis, 47*: 420–437. Reprinted by permission of Taylor & Francis, LLC.

## Notes

1 *Child analysis* or *child therapy* is usually undertaken after evaluating the child, which includes interviews with the parents (see Greenspan, 1981). These initial parent interviews allow an analyst to take a developmental history of the child, as well as gain impressions of the parent (or parents') personality (or personalities), the functioning of the couple (if there is one), and some sense of the family group dynamics. The analyst individually treats the child only if an internalized problem interferes with the child's progressive development.

2   The tradition in the United States has often, but not always, been that the child analyst or therapist treating the child also works with the parents. The tradition in the UK is that a separate therapist does the parent work (Sutton & Hughes, 2005). A full discussion of the advantages and disadvantages of these approaches is beyond the scope of this article. Analysts in the UK who regularly refer the parents to a separate therapist cite the greater privacy for the child work (see Altman, 2004: 194). Although there are doubtless advantages to that approach, I have often found my direct countertransference experiences of the parents (allowed when I am treating the child and conducting the collateral parent work) invaluable to my understanding of the adolescent.

3   In my own training, once-a-month meetings with parents were the norm, but this can vary for many reasons. Adolescents are often wary of parental involvement in their treatment. In this case, I would either meet infrequently with the parents or refer parents to a colleague for parent work. The seriousness of the parents' contributions to their adolescent's problems is another factor, as is their willingness to enter into parent work.

4   These developments were presented at a meeting of the American Psychoanalytic Association in 1971 and gave rise to two articles: 'Family organization and adolescent development' (Shapiro & Zinner, 1971), and 'Projective identification as a mode of perception and behavior in families of adolescents' (Zinner & Shapiro, 1972).

5   I could not locate any application of the major types of basic assumption functioning that Bion described (dependency, fight–flight, pairing) in either the object relations or the Tavistock family therapy literature.

6   It should be noted that although a variety of ethnicities and financial strata are represented in the cases discussed here, all are traditional, two-parent family structures. The absence of single-parent or gay-parented families reflects the case material I had available at the time of writing. Although Bion saw the potential for basic assumption functioning to be relevant to any group, it would be interesting to consider how the basic assumption modes might be differently manifested in nontraditional families. It strikes me that the way basic assumption pairing groups might function would be an interesting area for exploration.

## References

Altman, N. (2004). Child psychotherapy: Converging traditions. *Journal of Child Psychotherapy*, *30*: 189–206.

Alvarez, A. (1992). *Live Company*. London: Routledge.

Anderson, R. (1998). Suicidal behavior and its meaning in adolescence. In R. Anderson & A. Dartington (Eds.), *Facing It Out*. New York: Routledge, pp. 65–78.

Bion, W.R. (1961). *Experiences in Groups*. London: Tavistock.

Bion, W.R. (1967). Notes on memory and desire. *Psychoanalytic Forum, 2*: 271–280.

Bion, W.R. (2005a). *The Italian Seminars*. London: Karnac.

Bion, W.R. (2005b). *The Tavistock Seminars*. London: Karnac.

Brady, M. (2006). Review of *Working with Parents Makes Therapy Work* by Kerry Kelly Novick & Jack Novick. *fort da, 12*: 103–107.

Ferro, A. (2006). Unity of analysis: Similarities and differences in the analysis of children and grown-ups. *Psychoanalytic Quarterly, 75*: 477–500.

Fraiberg, S., Adelson, E., & Shapiro, V. (1975). Ghosts in the nursery: A psycho-analytic approach to the problems of impaired infant-mother relationships. *Journal of the American Academy of Psychiatry, 14*: 387–421.

Ganzarain, R. (1989). *Object Relations Group Psychotherapy*. Madison, CT: International Universities Press.

Graham, R. (1998). The heat of the moment: Psychoanalytic work with families. In R. Anderson & A. Dartington (Eds.), *Facing It Out*. New York: Routledge, pp. 143–158.

Greenspan, S. (1981). *The Clinical Interview of the Child*. New York: McGraw-Hill.

Kreeger, L. (1975). *The Large Group: Dynamics and Therapy*. Itasca, IL: F.E. Peacock.

Lawrence, W., Bain, A., & Gould, L. (1996). The fifth basic assumption. *Free Associations, 6*: 28–55.

Novick, K.K., & Novick, J. (2005). *Working with Parents Makes Therapy Work*. Northvale, NJ: Jason Aronson.

O'Shaughnessy, E. (1964). The absent object. *Journal of Child Psychotherapy, 1*(2): 34–43.

Ogden, T. (1982). *Projective Identification and Psychotherapeutic Technique*. Northvale, NJ: Jason Aronson.

Scharff, J.S. (1989). The development of object relations family therapy ideas. In J.S. Scharff (Ed.), *Foundations of Object Relations Family Therapy*. Northvale, NJ: Jason Aronson, pp. 3–22.

Shapiro, R.L. (1989). Family dynamics and object relations theory: An analytic, group-interpretive approach to family therapy. In J.S. Scharff (Ed.), *Foundations of Object Relations Family Therapy*. Northvale, NJ: Jason Aronson, pp. 225–245.

Shapiro, R.L. & Zinner, J. (1971). Family organization and adolescent development. In E. Miller (Ed.), *Task and Organization*. London: Wiley (1976), pp. 289–308.

Sutton, A., & Hughes, L. (2005). The psychotherapy of parenthood: Towards a formulation and valuation of concurrent work with parents. *Journal of Child Psychotherapy, 2*: 169–188.

Waddell, M. (1998). The scapegoat. In R. Anderson & A. Dartington (Ed.), *Facing It Out*. New York: Routledge, pp. 127–142.

Williams, G. (1998). Reflections on some particular dynamics of eating disorders. In R. Anderson & A. Dartington (Eds.), *Facing It Out*. New York: Routledge, pp. 79–88.

Zinner, J., & Shapiro, R.L. (1972). Projective identification as a mode of perception and behaviour in families of adolescents. *International Journal of Psychoanalysis*, *53*: 523–530.

# Index

For Product Safety Concerns and Information please contact our EU
representative GPSR@taylorandfrancis.com
Taylor & Francis Verlag GmbH, Kaufingerstraße 24, 80331 München, Germany